Thank you so much for everything. You have a lovely family. May the Lord bless you,

Harry, Ethelyn Abernethy

In famine He shall redeem thee

Job 5:20

Ph. 585-1818

240 Bush St. S
Salem. Or. 97302

Malcolm I. Forsberg

Author:
Land Beyond the Nile (Harper & Brothers)
Last Days on the Nile (J.B. Lippincott)
Dry Season (Sudan Interior Mission)

Edited by Kerry Lovering
Book Design by Charles J. Guth

In famine He shall redeem thee

**Famine relief and rehabilitation
in Ethiopia**

By Malcolm and Enid Forsberg

Published by Sudan Interior Mission

SUDAN INTERIOR MISSION

Australia:	P.O. Box 17, Summer Hill, N.S.W. 2130
Canada:	10 Huntingdale Blvd., Agincourt, Ontario M1W 1S9
Great Britain:	84 Beulah Hill, Upper Norwood, London SE19 3EP
New Zealand:	Institute Place, 427 Queen Street, Auckland 1
South Africa:	P.O. Box 64075, Highlands North, Johannesburg
Switzerland:	Chemin de la Fourmi 22, 1010 Lausanne
United States:	Cedar Grove, New Jersey 07009

First edition 1975
Library of Congress catalog number 75-2782

Printed and bound in Canada

Thank you so much for everything.

To the Sudan Interior Mission workers and their relief and rehabilitation partners, Ethiopian, Canadian, Australian, New Zealand, British, American, and Continental — a great team of dedicated Christians.

CONTENTS

vi

Of necessity

To tell the full story of the famine that ravaged so much of Africa in 1973-1974 would require several volumes. Of necessity, therefore, this account is limited. It focuses on one area only. It tells of some people only. It mentions some organizatiions only. But in fact, it is everybody's story, whether they are mentioned by name or not.

We wish there were some way to give recognition to every individual, every organization, every church, every group that participated in this great effort to meet the physical and spiritual needs of famine victims.

That is imposssible. But all who gave, and prayed, and worked, will find themselves in this story. We know they understand.

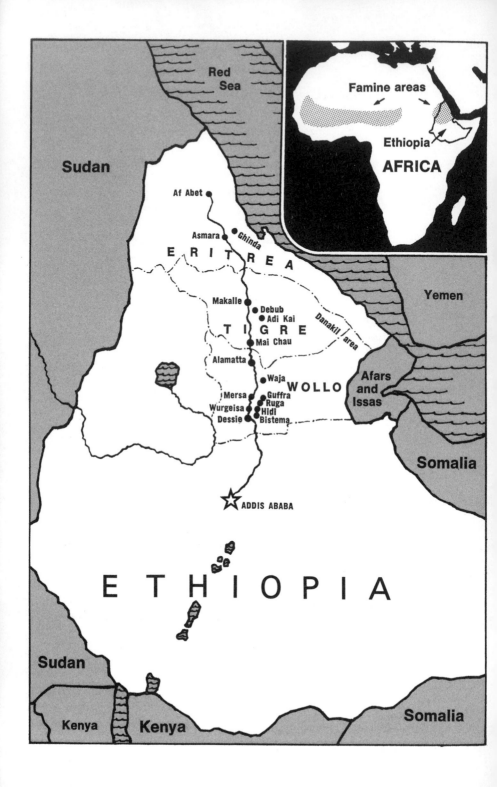

1. The road

There is a road that runs through northern Ethiopia. It writhes like a serpent through magnificent, tortuous mountains. It is the lifeline of the north, linking the capital city, Addis Ababa, which lies in the geographic center of the country, with Asmara, near the Red Sea.

As the crow flies, the distance between Addis Ababa and Asmara is 440 miles. As the road writhes, it is 668. In the summer of 1973 the road, the only one through the north, became a ribbon of hope, the dividing line between life and death, survival and starvation.

That summer was Ethiopia's dreadful time of hunger, the climax of a four-year drought that withered the north, drying up the land that slopes eastward toward the plains of the Red Sea coast. During that summer, gaunt with hunger, the people of the mountains left their homes, first in ones and twos, later in an overwhelming flood, and swarmed to the road, the only source of help they knew.

In the high altitudes of those mountains, reaching 15,000 feet in one place, the days are hot. The sun burns down, drawing sweat to the brow and baking the soil. But when it sets, the air chills. The nights are cold. At some seasons of the year it is not uncommon to find a shiver of ice on still water as the sun rises in the morning.

It is good land. The valleys are lush. The mountainsides, though rocky, produce well. In normal times the light rains come in February or March, although, being somewhat capricious, they may hold off until April. They soften the soil for plowing and planting, and early crops are put in.

In the hot and sunny days that follow, the grain sprouts and grows

1

rapidly. Some crops are ready for harvest before the heavy rains come, the torrential downpours that begin in late June or early July, depending, again, on the capriciousness of nature.

During the heavy rains the clouds unload their enormous cargo of water. The rain sheets down from leaden skies, filling the rivers till they boil and rage. At the height of the rainy season, two or three inches of rain may fall in a day. The people live in wetness. The thatch on their houses becomes sodden. Their clothes are damp. Their bare feet are cold as they tread the muddy paths. The cattle grow fat on the pasture, suddenly lush and green.

Almost daily, though, the sun shines. After the downpour, the sky clears and the welcome sun appears, warming the bones and cheering the heart.

Some time in September, as the days bring more and more sun and less and less rain, the farmers both plant and harvest. While the soil is wet and soft, they put in crops that mature quickly, that will grow enough while the soil has moisture to ripen in the dry weather that follows. By November, the year's crops are in. The granaries are full, and the people know that all is well.

Or so it was until the time of hunger. No one saw the trouble coming. It came gradually. And if they did sense trouble, they could not be sure when, or if, it really would arrive. And if it did arrive, there was nothing, apparently, that they could do.

If the light rains were late, or did not come at all, what could one do about it? One ate less, to be sure, but one lived in hope of an adequate crop after the next rains, the heavy ones. And if those rains were inadequate, and the fields produced little, what could one do about that? One ate even less, and felt weak, and became ill more easily, and sold a few possessions to buy food from the market.

Food was always there, of course. Some of it was brought from other parts of Ethiopia where there was no drought, and some from lands nearby that lay in more favored locations, places where the rain was adequate for some crop.

But of what use is food if one cannot buy it? So the men left home for a few weeks in hope of finding work in the towns along the great road. With money, they and their families could survive. Food was not the problem. Money was.

2. Ali

By the spring of 1973, Ali, a typical farmer who lived some 40 miles east of the road, was caught in the grip of the drought.

He looked over the field he had just plowed. It wasn't as rich and as damp as it should have been. Almost imperceptably, the rains had decreased in the last four years. His crops had become smaller and smaller. Would the time come, he wondered, when there would be insufficient food for his family and village?

Old men and women had told of times when food had been scarce, when the villagers had spent the days digging roots or threshing grass. The roots and grass seed had not given much nourishment. Springs and streams had dried up. The village women had to walk a long way to fill their pots with water.

That kind of drought had not occurred in Ali's village in his lifetime. But he was apprehensive now. He did not have much land, and he needed all it could produce. His father and grandfather had farmed here. When his grandfather died, the land had been divided among his three sons. The pieces of land had grown even smaller when Ali's father and brothers divided it among their sons. But what could one do?

Ali had learned to hitch up the oxen and plow when he was less than ten years old. During this farming season, as in the past, he had hitched the two oxen together with the yoke and carried the wooden plow to the field on his shoulder. All day long he stumbled over the clods, lashing the sides of the oxen with his leather whip, or cracking it over their heads. The oxen jerked and staggered as they slowly

3

stirred up a few yards of rocky soil.

"My oxen are like me," Ali said to himself. "They are thin and hungry and there is little to feed them."

In the late afternoon he untied the plow from the yoke, and put both yoke and plow on his shoulder as he drove the oxen homeward. He went by way of the watering place, for the oxen were thirsty.

Ali and his neighbors had made a small dam with stones and branches, to form a drinking place in the stream bed. The water was just a trickle now, muddy from its trip down the mountainside from the little spring.

When the oxen had drunk, they nibbled at the dry grass along the edge of the shriveled watercourse while Ali discussed oxen, crops, rainfall, and village happenings with his neighbors.

Life had been this way from the day of Ali's first plowing. Now he was a man with a wife and five children to care for. Each year for the last four seasons the crops had been smaller. Each year there was less water in the stream. The sun seemed hotter. His wife and children had grown thin. They never had quite enough to eat. Still, Ali and his people planted in hope. Rain had always come, even though it had been late, or not as much as hoped for.

He had a few goats and sheep and chickens, and two cows. Food for the animals had grown scarce as the grass dried up. Once beautiful and lush, his village on the mountainside was now dry. The granite rocks stuck out in defiance. The sloping fields were brown.

Three hour's walk from Ali's home, beyond three separate ridges, lay the town and the market. To get there was a nine-hour excursion. Three hours on the path, three hours in the market, and three long hours back over the trail. Local farmers made the trip weekly, even when they had little or nothing to trade. The market was part of their social life. It was there they learned the news of the nation and the world. Traders from distant parts, even as far away as the north-south road, brought their wares and told of what was happening. These traders brought salt, cloth, peppers, spices, hoes, baskets, and thread for weaving. They brought oxen for plowing and donkeys for hauling produce.

At this time of year, with grain supplies gone, the farmers brought sheep and goats and chickens to trade or sell for other food.

Ali started off for the market with one of his goats. He joined the flow of neighbors winding among the rocks and thorn bushes. Generations of his ancestors had shuffled over these paths, and now there were deep ruts in the sandstone.

The sun was hot at eleven o'clock when the trail gave way to flat, brown paddocks bisected by the wide, well-traveled dirt road leading to the market. Ali could see the few large trees that marked the location.

There were a few shops on the edge of the market area. Signs advertising various products were nailed to the mud and wattle walls. Some of them were old, advertising products that were no longer available. Even in this out-of-the-way place there were Coca Cola signs. But Ali could not read. Not that it mattered. The sweet liquid in the bottles was too expensive for him. The brewed or distilled products of his own countrymen were more stimulating than the bottled stuff. But he had no money for that now, either. Ali was a Muslim, and Muslims traditionally do not drink intoxicating beverages, but Ali and his people did not let their religion deprive them of their beer.

The market itself consisted of brush shelters which gave some protection from the sun, but none from the rain. They were used only once a week. The rest of the time they stood gaunt and empty. A stranger passing by would not have guessed that on one day of the week the deserted flatland and its shacks would be alive with thousands of people.

Villagers who had goods to sell set up shop according to their products. Under a large sycamore tree sat the sellers of home brew, produced from barley. Ali noted that the number of beer merchants had greatly decreased. The drought had reduced the amount of barley available.

The principal crops from the higher areas were barley and wheat. In the lowlands the people cultivated sorghum, corn, and teff, a grass-like grain peculiar to Ethiopia. Teff was used almost exclusively to make one of the national foods, *injera,* a large pancake-like bread. Injera was served with *wat,* a stew that was made in many ways. There was chicken wat, and beef, and mutton. Sometimes it was made only of vegetables, especially for the fast days of the Orthodox church, when it was forbidden to eat animal products. The wat was heavily seasoned with red pepper and spices.

In normal times Ali had driven a donkey to the market, laden with barley. With the money it brought he bought a load of teff for making injera. His wife ground the fine white seeds into flour and made a thin batter, which she baked on a large clay griddle. Under the griddle was a crackling fire, fed with twigs and dry grass and even dried cow dung. The dung would have served a better purpose had it been returned to the land, but Ali had never been taught about that.

While Ali led his goat through the market, he noticed that although the piles of produce sold by the local people were small, the merchants had plenty of grain to offer. The drought was not affecting everybody the same way, Ali knew. Some were reasonably well off, as usual. Some were better off, he realized bitterly, because they did not grow grain, they bought and sold it.

In times of drought they brought grain in from other places, and raised the price higher and higher, knowing there was no other source of supply. Not only had the price of teff gone away up, but the price of goats and barley had gone down. Ali was to learn that it costs more to starve than to eat well.

He had always been suspicious of the merchants, though. They were well dressed, had plenty to eat, and were housed under corrugated iron roofs which did not have to be replaced every few years as did his thatch.

The merchants always had reasons for this inequality. They had to haul their goods on trucks, they explained, and fuel was expensive. The trucks were always breaking down and repairs were costly. Ali had only a vague idea about these matters. Whatever happened about trucks and crops, the merchant was always better off than the farmer.

Ali hoped to sell his goat for at least five dollars. He and his family could eat the meat, but it would not last long. Grain would last much longer. He offered the animal in the area where goats and sheep were crowded together. He got into bargaining sessions with several buyers but none offered five dollars.

The only real offer he had was from a merchant who said he would take it for one dollar. Ali shuddered. A dollar would buy very little teff. He was tempted to take the goat back home, but he could not bear to have his family go without injera until next market day. Whether buying or selling, he was the loser.

Ali had no choice. He sold his goat for a dollar. He bought less than one-fifth the usual amount of teff a goat should have brought, and started on his weary way home. He had eaten nothing all day, nor had those who walked with him. They were all from the same area, where drought had reduced them all to poverty. They had nothing with which to buy the prepared foods vended in the market. They had only one subject of conversation as they plodded along... drought and hunger in their villages, plenty of food and high prices in the market.

They had heard no talk of mercy. No one had proposed lowering prices to help the victims of drought. There were suggestions that farmers should sell their oxen and plows to those who were better off. But how would they grow another crop without oxen and plows when the rains returned? Still, for the present, they had to eat, and there was teff in the market.

It was almost dark when Ali arrived at the door of his hut. He greeted his wife, Maryam, softly.

Maryam and her children knew that Ali would not have much in his hand when he returned from the market. But they were too tired and hungry to say much about the pitifully small amount of grain he brought.

"I was given only one dollar for the goat," Ali mumbled. "And the price of teff has gone up. We will use up this little bag of grain long before the next market day."

And what about the wat? It would not be meat wat for some time, but Maryam had a few chick peas and a bit of pepper and spice that she had grown. The bread would not be entirely dry as they ate it. They could use a chicken, of course, but then there would be one less chicken to ward off hunger in the uncertain days ahead. And chicken wat, to be good, would need rancid butter, and onions. It would be better to keep it for a feast day in the future. Besides, it was a scrawny bird now. Even the grasshoppers seemed scarce, and Maryam was careful to see that grain did not drop to the ground from her grinding stones. In better times the chickens flocked around whenever she was grinding, picking up the bits that fell.

Normally, Ali and his neighbors were loquacious. They told stories around the fires. They spread news as fast as it happened. They joked and they gossiped. They talked about animals and crops. Now conversation had almost died out.

During good times when the rains came, there was planning. Where shall we plant the barley this year? Where shall we plant the wheat? Why not grow a patch of potatoes? This would be a good year for broad beans. The brightness of conversation had gone. Hunger had dulled the spirits. It had even dulled the appetite.

Ali's wife had kept a few bits of injera from the previous day's meal. She brought these out and each had a mouthful or two. It was dark now. There were coals in the fireplace between the three stones. At least there was fuel.

But there was little water. Maryam would have to leave at dawn again with her six-gallon clay pot on her back to bring home water. It would take nearly two hours to get to the spring. She would have to wait her turn, for the water was running very slowly. She would join the other women in the conversation... about water shortage and hunger.

Her little daughter usually went with her, carrying her little jug, learning from her mother the duties of the household.

There was some comfort in being at the spring. All the women were in the same predicament. All were hungry. All suffered the agony of having little to give their families. There is a kind of cold comfort in the unity of tragedy.

It was eight o'clock the next morning before there were signs of life in Ali's village. The animals in the corral had hardly stirred. They were hungry and thirsty, but there was no reason to bellow, bleat, or baa. Only the lone rooster welcomed the day with a half-hearted crow.

This was a new experience for Ali and his people. They had always been active. Lethargy was something they had not known. Now there was a lethargy of body and mind. They did not cry out for help. Had they done so, no one would have heard.

3. Famine!

Along the great north-south road lie three SIM stations. Coming in from the north, from the large and spacious city of Asmara, one drives 235 miles south to Mai Chau. Mai Chau is a small place. The SIM site there has only a school, a clinic, and two missionary dwellings.

Driving south another 35 miles brings one to Alamatta, which is much like Mai Chau.

Continuing south another 150 miles, through towns with names like Mersa and Wurgeisa, that cluster along the road like beads on a string, one comes to Dessie. Nine miles outside of Dessie is the SIM site, known as Bora Meda.

Bora Meda is large. There is a school there, and a Bible training center, and a hospital. There is a treatment center for leprosy patients. It is headquarters for an extensive public health service and an equally extensive leprosy control program.

From Dessie to Addis Ababa is 250 miles, not a great distance in some circumstances, but great enough to separate two worlds in others. It was at Bora Meda in the spring of 1973 that the fact of famine became known to SIM.

At Bora Meda there had been no lack of rain. The place was like a garden. A herd of 50 beautiful cattle grazed contentedly on the tender grass. A flock of sheep moved up and down the rich pasture land keeping fat and satisfied. SIM missionaries had many acres of grain and vegetables under cultivation, most of it used to feed the leprosy patients who were cared for on the station.

There may have been talk of drought in some parts of northern

Ethiopia, but Bora Meda was not one of them.

The missionary in charge of evangelism at Bora Meda was Les Unruh, a Nebraska farmer-preacher who was helping 50 Ethiopian evangelists from other parts of the country, mainly from Wallamo in the south, spread the gospel across a wide area of south Wollo province. They had been selected and sent by their home churches and were very much missionaries in their own right.

They lived in the mountains around Dessie, using Bora Meda as their base. They came in to Bora Meda regularly, for teaching and encouragement, and to report on their work. South Wollo province, like most of the north, was mainly Islamic or Orthodox (Coptic) in persuasion, and the evangelists did not report many conversions. But they established their presence and sowed the seed, and were confident that in God's good time the harvest would come.

The dynamo of the Bora Meda staff was Dr. Dietrich Schmoll of West Germany. He had studied medicine there, and then served a term with SIM in Ethiopia. Blond and sturdy, Dr. Schmoll was also compassionate and indefatigable. New ideas for carrying on his work came to him daily. He put his ideas into practice as rapidly as they came to mind.

"It isn't enough to heal sick people this year then treat the same people for the same diseases next year," he maintained. "We need to set up a system of public health stations so that we can *prevent* disease."

So Dietrich Schmoll, his wife, Ruth, and children, did not go to Germany for their furlough. They went to USA, to Baltimore, Maryland, where Schmoll enrolled in a Master's course in Public Health at Johns Hopkins University. He returned to Ethiopia ready to go.

"We have to get a corps of Christian Ethiopians together and train them in the basics of public health work and send them out," he announced to his wife. Ruth was not surprised. She had heard little else but public health for the last five years.

Most of Dr. Schmoll's health workers were recruited from the same southern church areas from which Unruh's evangelists had come. When they arrived, the training course was held with emphasis on the prevention and treatment of leprosy.

Soon Dr. Schmoll's public health workers, too, were spread out over south Wollo. Like the evangelists, they returned periodically for supplies, salary, and refresher courses. Things were working well.

There were over 7,000 leprosy patients under their care.

It was these men, the evangelists and the public health workers, who sounded the alarm about the effects of the drought. They lived in the villages, some of them remote, and they knew what was happening.

"Hunger is increasing," they said, on one of their visits to Bora Meda. They described the condition they were beginning to see... ribs easily counted on gaunt bodies, contradicted by stomachs swollen from the effects of hunger.

Dr. Schmoll was concerned. He expressed his concern to the local authorities and to everyone who would listen. "Something will have to be done," he told them. Some things were done, but in Wollo what was done was too little and too late.

Perhaps there was some excuse. The valleys and gorges and mountain slopes in themselves confused the reports of drought and its effects. Beyond one ridge there was enough rain to grow a crop. Beyond the next there was none.

Altitude, air currents, the jumble of mountain geography made an intricate pattern of farming procedures. Farmers did not all sow at the same time, or reap, even though they were in sight of each other. Food supplies varied with the area concerned. Some people were not hungry at all. Some were hungry, but not starving. Others were weak and near death.

When truth and rumor conflict, and no one is quite sure of what to do, and the wheels of legislation turn slowly, at best, it is easier to wait and see what will happen than to lay plans and be prepared.

In Wollo, they waited too long. The dam burst almost without warning. Hungry villagers stayed in their homes until the last crumb was gone. They had no reason to leave. If they were going to die, they preferred to die at home.

Then the word began to spread, partly true, that there was help along the road. With nothing to lose, they clutched at this last hope.

The first wave of famine victims appeared almost without notice. Suddenly there were people along the road, begging from passing traffic. The main streets of the towns began to fill with the pathetic forms of villagers looking for help that was not there.

Dr. Schmoll's workers brought him the word.

"People are coming into the towns all along the road," they said. "Some of them just lie along the road. They are weak. They die."

These men had seen extreme physical distress in many of the

leprosy-afflicted people they treated. They were accustomed to sorrow and death. But they had seen more than they could bear in the towns along the road. "Oh, trouble! Oh, sorrow!" they cried out in their language. "It is getting worse every day," they reported. "It is like a river in the rainy season. First there is little, then there is much. And there is more to come."

All the reports indicated that the hungry people were coming from the east of the road.

"Where is it worst?" Dr. Schmoll asked.

"Around Wurgeisa," they replied.

"That's about 60 miles," Dr. Schmoll said.

He turned to Les. "Will you come with me?" Les nodded.

They jumped into the Leprosy Control vehicle and soon disappeared among the eucalyptus trees at the base of the mountain.

It took Dr. Schmoll and Les Unruh less than two hours to go to Wurgeisa. It usually takes longer than that. But they had a sense of impending disaster.

The men had been over the winding mountainous road to Wurgeisa often. In the towns, and even along the road, they had always been approached by beggars. They had given coins to some. It was a common thing.

When they approached Wurgeisa, however, they gasped. Nothing they had heard prepared them for what they saw. There were crowds of people in the main street of the town. There was a pathetic uniformity in their dress — all were in gray rags. Some were barely covered. Most of the children had but one cloth, which was thrown across their shoulders.

When Dr. Schmoll stopped his car, it was completely surrounded by begging people. But these were not the beggars he had seen before. These were mostly women with children.

The men jumped from the car. They stopped to examine some of the figures lying motionless by the edge of the road. They were inert, many of them, having passed into that twilight of death where hunger, food, and famine no longer matter. Babies lay by their mothers. It was difficult in some cases to determine whether either or both was dead.

The words rang in the missionaries' ears, "Oh trouble, oh sorrow!"

Schmoll and Unruh were men of action. They gave orders, they laid out programs, they got things done. But when they saw hundreds of people dying before their eyes, they were stopped in their tracks. "God, help us," Les prayed silently.

"Let's see what the rest of the town looks like," Dr. Schmoll suggested. He was in the car before he finished the sentence.

As they drove, they saw a stretcher carried on the shoulders of four men. "He is dead," someone stated. "They are carrying the dead to the grave. About 20 die each day."

The people who lived in Wurgeisa had plenty to eat. The men were strong. They had been ordered by their chief to dig large graves and to put the bodies in it.

As Schmoll and Unruh stared at the incredible scene, their anger grew. "Such a thing should never be allowed to happen!" Schmoll roared. "Thousands of people must be affected by this drought! I'm heading back to Dessie to tell the provincial officials what we have seen. I can't believe they know nothing about this horrible situation!"

As they turned the car around and headed back down the road, a bread delivery truck stopped in front of a small store. Schmoll stopped the car and the two men jumped out. They went to the store, and bought the whole truckload.

When they stepped out onto the street, they were swamped. Very quickly the bread buns were being fed to children and devoured by adults.

Dietrich Schmoll was a man of intense feelings. He wanted to put food into the mouths of the starving right now. Much of his feeling was transmitted to the accelerator. The road at that point is surfaced with stones. It winds around the mountains, up and down hill, ofttimes with eucalyptus groves lining the road. It was not built for men of strong feeling who were bent on urgent business.

It was late afternoon when the two men burst into the office of the provincial medical officer in Dessie. The officials there were accustomed to having Schmoll arrive in a flurry.

"There is famine in the mountains east of Wurgeisa," he declared bluntly. "People are coming into town by the hundreds, begging for food. Some are dying. We must get food there, immediately."

The official's cool response raised Schmoll's temperature. Schmoll knew that the official, like all officials, was trapped in government procedural channels. He did not doubt the official's concern, for he had seen that concern demonstrated on other occasions when the welfare of the people was at stake, but the fact that he did not *do* something bothered Schmoll.

"Let us go see my superior," the man said. "We have heard similar reports before, and we are aware of what we call 'the difficulty,' but things must be done through the proper channels."

Schmoll was not inclined to wait for conferences in government offices. He and Les went back to the car and drove to Bora Meda. He was soon on the phone in his home, talking to SIM headquarters in Addis Ababa.

"There is terrible famine here in Wollo province," he almost shouted. "Find grain and send it to Wurgeisa at once. I don't know where you'll get the money, but buy it anyway. And write a letter to the provincial office here in Dessie and tell them about the reports we have. Tell them 20 people a day are dying in Wurgeisa. Maybe if *you* write they'll listen."

SIM was in action. They did not realize how big a job they had undertaken. That was the way it began, in late April 1973.

4. The survey

News of famine began to flow in from several sources. Missions and churches were concerned. What could they do? In May 1973 several organizations got together for informal discussion. SIM missionary Don Stilwell, a pharmacist serving as SIM Medical Secretary in Ethiopia, represented SIM. He had been with SIM for 15 years.

Don didn't know it, but he was taking on the job of relief coordinator for SIM's part in the enormous task that lay ahead.

The first step, Don reported after the discussions, was to get some facts. SIM assigned him that task. Don looked around for a partner, and was given Ken Radach. It was a good choice.

Ken had served with SIM since 1949, first in southeastern Sudan, then in Ethiopia near the Sudan border, then with relief and rehabilitation work in southern Sudan following the end of the civil war there. He had recently come to Addis Ababa with his wife, Gloria, for a new assignment. This one fitted him like a glove.

Don and Ken took off for the north immediately on a quick survey trip. The report they would make on their return would shape the direction that SIM would go. Some of their conclusions and recommendations showed remarkable insight into what was then a very clouded picture. God obviously guided them.

What they had heard, they found to be true. There were relief measures in action in some areas. Government was working, but slowly. Local officials often expressed frustration with the central government. Some were alert to the situation and doing what they could with what they could procure. But nowhere were the measures adequate.

They stopped at one place where UNICEF milk was being mixed and given to infants, and small portions of meal were being distributed. It was a daily distribution scheme, with about 300 people receiving help.

"The area looked like a desert," they reported. "No grass, no crops. Most of the cattle have died, and anthrax has come into the area, combining with drought to kill the animals."

One official at Dessie seemed very weary from months of struggle with drought and its consequences. He had obtained donations from businessmen in the town and used it to help needy people who gathered there. Ten of the 12 districts in Wollo Province were affected, he said. Many men had left their wives and children to go to different parts of Ethiopia looking for work. This had left an inordinately large number of women and children and aged people in the famine area.

They pushed on to Alamatta. "This area has not had rain for three years," they reported. "Up to 8000 people have gathered in Alamatta town at one time looking for help. These are hanging around in the streets and market, on people's verandas, and in the government compound, hoping for some kind of aid. We saw a lot of very hungry people there, predominantly women and children. Officials told us that an average of 12 people die of starvation every day. We are not convinced that these figures are accurate, but it is beyond doubt that some are starving to death or dying from diseases that result from malnutrition. It is evident that children are suffering. Marasmus (deficiency of protein and carbohydrates) is rampant, and 50 percent of the children show symptoms of bronchitis. Many have eye infections such as trachoma."

They found, as Ali had, that the price of grain had gone up. "During harvest season," they reported, "the price of one quintal (220 pounds)* of teff was as low as $6.50. During the present time it is as high at $15.00. Sorghum was as low as $4.00, but is now up to $12.50."

People had sold their cattle to buy grain. Previously, the price of one animal would buy up to five quintals (1100 pounds) of grain. "Now," they reported, "the sale of an animal will realize only 40 — 50 pounds of grain. Animals of late have been selling for $5.00 or less."

The cattle were in a pitiful condition. Oxen that were still strong enough to plow sold for $10.00 to $15.00.

They found famine conditions prevalent as far north as Mai Chau.

On their return trip they found a critical situation had developed in Dessie during their week's absence. "Funds and grain have been exhausted," they wrote. "Thousands of people are coming in to look for help. The government was forced to act by sending these people home. This is no easy thing, but the transport companies cooperated and helped carry people back to the area of their village, where possible. Some 6000 people were transported, and promised grain in their home areas. Local relief funds provided about 10 quarts of grain per family, and the health centers gave milk and porridge to children."

What happened at Dessie was a foretaste of what would happen all up and down the great road in the next few weeks. Villagers stayed on their land until they could stay no longer. Then they swarmed to the towns in unpredictable waves, each day multiplying the number of destitute who appeared as from nowhere.

Don and Ken made their recommendations. They had good cooperation from local officials in their survey, and were supplied with statistics. In the two provinces of Wollo and Tigre, there were an estimated one and a half *million* persons affected.

"We agree with the government report," they stated, "that in spite of present efforts, the famine situation is rapidly getting worse and is spreading. Indeed, the scale of the problem has reached such proportions that prompt and adequate assistance has to be obtained to meet the immediate requirements of the famine-stricken areas."

Their observation concerning the method of food distribution was extremely significant: "The method of distributing in large centers is unsatisfactory. It leads to large-scale migration away from the villages, creating a floating society dependent on donations. Without proper housing they are vulnerable to infection and contagious disease. We feel that SIM is in a position to correct this problem by working in the villages as much as possible. It will take manpower, but the communities involved, we feel, will rise to the occasion and cooperate in creating a stable community in spite of famine."

They took a careful look into the future, and came up with observations that would have to be implemented as soon as the immediate need was met. "There must be long-term projects so this cycle will not repeat itself. Possibilities include relocating some people, teaching different types of farming, introducing cash crops other than grain, exploring irrigation possibilities, introducing anti-erosion schemes such as reforestation, and encouraging light industry for diversification."

There were three things, however, that had to be done immediately.

One was to get food, clothing, and medicine to the victims.

Two was to start food-for-work programs so that men would stay at home in their villages.

Three was to provide seed grain to replace what had been eaten, and help the people sow their fields once again with the first prospect of rain.

On paper it looked good. It was a different thing to put it into action. Where would the personnel come from to do all that needed doing? Where would the money come from?

Disaster was about to multiply. The victims of starvation could not wait.

*Ethiopia uses the metric system for weights, measures, and currency.

5.   Flight

The rains did not come. Ali and Maryam watched as their means of livelihood disintegrated around them. One by one, they sold or ate their few animals and chickens.

They even sold the oxen, and one of the cows. The price they brought crushed Ali's soul. True, the animals were thin and weak, but, given food, they would flesh out again. Someone would make great gain at his expense, Ali knew. The grain he bought with the money had a taste of bitterness in his mouth.

Ali and Maryam clung to their home longer than most of the people in the villages nearby. The family grew thin and listless, and the younger children whimpered, but they could not bring themselves to leave. Bad as things were, surely, they reasoned, home was better than the unknown.

Rumors had been strong about food and shelters. Many had gone to see if the rumors were true. The government, it was said, with the help of some foreigners, had built shelters along the great road. Those who entered the shelters were given free food.

"We hear so many rumors," Ali said to his wife. "The wise man at Waji was going to make it rain, for a price. We each gave him a goat. The rain did not come. Then Diboli offered to buy our land, but the price he offered wasn't worth considering. Why do such men always want so much for so little?"

Ali and Maryam endlessly debated the wisdom of leaving. Were there people in the world who really cared enough to give free food to anyone who needed it? Were there really shelters? Or was it a trick?

As the word about the shelters grew stronger, more of Ali's neighbors disappeared. But none of them came back to say, "We have found grain. It is as we heard."

But then, Ali pondered, if people found grain, why would they return home? There was none here.

The prospect of bitter disappointment if the rumors turned out to be false held Ali to his land. There was a greater feeling of security to be had in one's own house than in wandering far away.

When it was apparent that the rains had failed, Maryam began to cook the little hoard of seed grain they had saved. "It will keep us alive a little longer," Ali said. There was desperation in his voice. Hope was nearly gone.

The night the last cow died decided the issue. They had tried to take it to market, but it was too weak to walk that far. "We will watch her carefully," Ali said, "and when we see that she is dying, we will butcher her. The meat will give us a few meals."

They waited one day too long. The cow died during the night, tethered just inside the door of their house. It was the custom to keep the animals inside. They were safe there, and their body heat provided welcome warmth in the cold nights.

In the morning, Ali and Maryam looked at the dead animal and sighed. They took hold of the legs and tried to drag it outside. They could not. They did not have the strength.

"It is the end," Ali said, finally. "There are unbelievers who would eat the flesh of an animal that has died of itself, but we will not. It is not the will of Allah. We must try to find the shelter. And we must leave tomorrow, before the beast begins to rot. May Allah help us."

Ali and his family had seldom gone anywhere other than to market. Even Ali had not been much farther from home than that. There had been no need. To look for the shelter was to journey into the unknown. Ali looked at the mountain ridges to the west. Somewhere out there was their last and only hope.

"We do not know how far it is," he commented, anxiety in his voice.

"It does not matter," Maryam replied, with dull finality. "If we die on the road it will not matter for you and me. For us, it is the end. This is our village, our home. To be buried in our home soil is more important than to live on some other person's soil far away. But there are the children. They can start life over again. The far country will become theirs. For their sakes we must go."

She began preparation for the journey. She ground and baked the little grain that remained, so it could be eaten along the road. What would the road be like, she wondered? Would they have to cross a desert? Beyond the ridges of home, all was hostility, she and Ali had heard. People who had guns, and whose purpose was to rob strangers were out there somewhere. But surely robbers would not want to bother their little family? Ali had sold his knives, his plow, his axe, his spears, and even his adze. There was nothing to take.

That last night at home, they killed and ate the straggly rooster. It would give them strength to start off early in the morning.

Maryam tied the children's ragged clothes around them, and gave each one a small gourd of water. She carried the baby on her back in a leather sling decorated with cowrie shells. Ali had a gourd of water slung on a stick over his shoulder. The food was wrapped in rags and carried on the back of the oldest boy. The other children also carried a small amount of roasted barley, all that was left in the house.

There was a trace of light shining from behind them as they made their way down the mountains and to the west. But soon the sun was up. It burned down upon them as they reached the lowlands. The children were the first to ask for water, as they stopped under the shade of a large cactus plant. Ali gave each one a small amount in the hope that they would find more along the way. They moved on. The children were soon tired, but their parents encouraged them to keep going. A little food helped them.

The baby, sleeping much of the time, was getting heavier on Maryam's back. When the three-year-old cried with weariness, Ali stooped down and let her climb on his back. At any other time this would have been shameful. Men in his tribe did not carry children. Certainly not on their backs. But the custom did not matter now.

"How far can we go?" Ali asked, not expecting a reply. "The children are so tired already. But we must endure," he added. The baby was crying more frequently now, and stops had to be made more and more often.

Later in the afternoon, they saw the thatched roofs of a small village on a hillside.

"Perhaps we will find people," Maryam said, mustering a little excitement in her voice to encourage the children. But when they reached the village, no one was there.

"They have gone to look for the shelter, too," Maryam said. She pointed through the cactus fence to several new graves. In Islamic custom, they were covered with stones. "Some of the people may return," she added. "Some will not."

"It is like our village," Ali reflected. "There are no cows, no people, no animals, even the grass has been pulled from some of the roofs. I do not like the graves. There are more here than in our village."

They decided to spend the night there. They rested in the shade of one of the houses, passing around and emptying another gourd of water. They each took a small portion of the now-dried injera. They did not eat it hastily, for hunger had created restraint in such a family. The baby had much of Maryam's portion, before dropping off into a deep sleep. The village was about 2000 feet lower than what they were used to, which made it feel warmer. Soon they were all asleep, lying on the ground, covered only with their rags.

Again, the first streaks of light awakened them. They took their small pile of injera pieces, and started out. Weariness came earlier than it had yesterday. The older children were falling behind now, too, and the parents had to rest more often. From time to time they met other travelers on the path, but there was little conversation with those who greeted them. They all knew what was happening. There was nothing to say.

Toward noon they ascended yet another mountain ridge. It took a number of hours to reach the top of the pass. The steep mule path was often left behind in favor of those which were longer, but gave easier ascent. Ali realized that they were no longer meeting other travelers. Somewhere they had left the main path and were wandering alone. "Perhaps it will not matter," Ali thought. "We do not know where to go in any case." As the afternoon sun beat upon them Maryam turned to Ali.

"Can you see the baby? She seems so quiet."

Ali looked at the tiny figure on Maryam's back.

"Stop!" he said, a tremble in his voice. "Untie her."

As Maryam loosened the leather straps, Ali lifted out the limp little body. Together they examined their child. The other children sensed what had happened.

"We will come to a village soon," Ali said hopefully. "We will bury her there. I do not want to bury her in the wilderness."

He placed the baby's body on Maryam's back again and she secured the straps once more across her breasts. The family walked silently down the mountain, stumbling over the rocks, as tears coursed down the mother's cheeks.

In the late afternoon they came in sight of a small plateau. "There will be villages here," Ali said. There were villages, but they were deserted.

"They, too, have gone to the shelter," Maryam said. "And there are new graves here, too."

"We must bury our baby before dark," Ali said softly. He hunted for a forgotten hoe, or a pointed stick, anything he could dig with. There was nothing. Finally, he pulled a pointed stick from a roof. "This will have to do," he said wearily.

The clay was dry and hard. Ali pried clods loose and piled them up. He had hardly made a start when his strength gave out. "I must rest," he said.

His nine-year-old son picked up the stick, and lifted a few pieces of dirt. They took turns off and on, strengthened by a little food and water.

Maryam sat close by, her baby on her lap. Would they have to leave their baby to the hyenas, she wondered, seeing the slow progress Ali and her son were making? She shuddered at the thought. Soon fatigue overcame her, as it had the children. She and they slept in the shade of the ever-present cactus. The usual prickly pear fruit of the cactus was missing this year, or they would have eaten it.

Ali watched his wife and children with apprehension. They had been strangely silent most of the day. Those who died of hunger passed through this silent period in which nothing mattered, Ali knew. Ali could scarcely dig one small grave. How could he dig another?

He returned to his task, stabbing at the soil with almost child-like effort.

It was midnight before he decided the grave was deep enough. Maryam was now lying on her back sound asleep, or comatose. Ali did not wake her. He picked up the baby from beside her, wrapped it in a torn piece of cloth, and gently laid it in the hole. He crushed the clods as best he could, and spread the soil carefully over the body. He had no strength to find stones to mark the spot. With a sob he made his way to Maryam's side and lay down next to the wall of the empty hut.

When he was awakened by the children next morning, Ali wondered if he had slept at all. His body felt as though it had had no rest. His first thought was of his unfinished task.

He looked for rocks to cover the grave. He quickly discovered that carrying them was almost too much for him. "Maybe twelve will be enough," he thought. "It is a small grave."

On completing the task he tried to say his Islamic prayers. But how could he wash his hands and feet, when most of the water was gone? "Allah!" he cried out in his extremity. At least he could call the name.

Maryam stirred, as out of a bad dream. She felt beside her for her baby, but there was nothing there. She arose on her elbow, and saw her husband moving among the mounds of stones, and remembered.

The four children sat nearby, patiently holding the cloth containing the injera crumbs. Together the family finished their last bit of food and drank a little water. Ali could hardly swallow his few crumbs.

"Come," he said. "Let us go."

They struggled up, and forced themselves to walk. They went on as in a daze now, passing the three-year-old from one to another, each one helping her walk a little way. For a while, they joined a large group of other refugees, but could not keep up with them. They fell behind. They did not remember how many hills they passed over, or how many times they sat down. The stream beds were all dry, and their thirst grew.

Hope of reaching the mysterious shelter was dimming.

"What will happen to the children if Maryam and I die?" Ali thought. The thought increased his determination to press on, if determination could help him at this point.

The country was dry and dusty, with barren fields and odd, empty houses. Birds were almost absent. Skeletons of animals lay near the path. Ali realized that they had lost the path again, but there was nothing to do except plod along toward the west.

About noon they came down into a broad valley, with some trees among recently cultivated fields. They had not walked far when they came to a road.

Was this their road of hope? It didn't look like much, gray and dusty, and covered with gravel. There were no people in sight, no signs or sounds of life. Ali studied the gray dust, and recognized truck wheel marks such as he had seen at the valley market. Would another truck come along that road? Would it stop to help them?.

Ali did not know. But he knew they could go no farther. "If this is not it," he thought, "we are dead."

They found a place to rest in the shade of a tree, on the shoulder of the road. In a short time they were all in deep sleep.

1. A dejected Ethiopian farmer keeps vigil by the roadside over his dying ox. In some areas, 80% of the cattle died.

2. Dr. Schmoll talks with neighbors at Bora Meda. Public health workers under Schmoll's charge alerted SIM to the crisis.

3. Refugees arriving at an SIM relief center show workers the only food they had — edible weeds.

4. L to R: Les Unruh, SIM evangelism coordinator at Bora Meda; Ken Radach, SIM field coordinator of relief; Don Stilwell, SIM administrative coordinator of relief.

5. Gaunt and tattered, mothers and children wait passively for medical treatment at Wurgeisa clinic.

6. Distributing Fafa, a high protein, easily-digested gruel, at Alamatta.

7. Swollen with edema, which often accompanies malnutrition, a child whose parents have died arrives at the makeshift orphanage at Wurgeisa.

8. Mary Amalia cares for victims at Mersa. The man (L) is receiving IV drip.

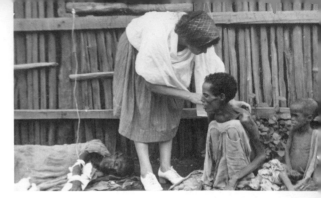

9. Volunteer Myron Jesperson helps unload a truckload of grain.

10. In the large storehouse built at Alamatta, grain is paid to wives of food-for-work laborers.

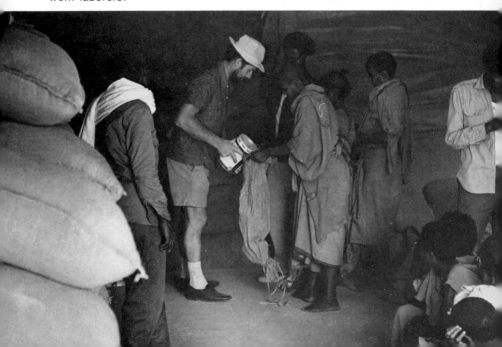

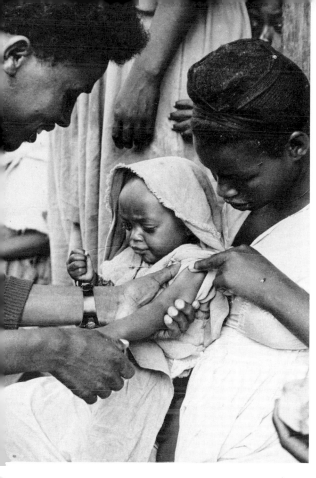

11. An Ethiopian dresser prepares a child for inoculation. Vaccination was used to prevent spread of disease.

12. A cholera victim receives intravenous infusion to replace lost body fluids. Minutes often made the difference between life and death.

13. Nearly dead from starvation, a lad named Girma Makonnen lies in the shade of a tree at Alamatta waiting for treatment.

14. Girma Makonnen, one year later, with SIM nurse Chris Ott.

15. A child who had been taken for burial, then found to be alive.

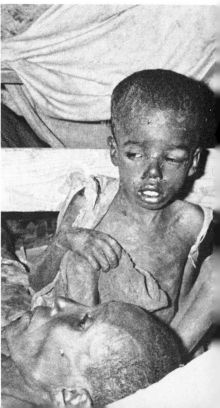

16. Over 200 children crowd into temporary school set up by relief and rehabilitation (R&R) workers at Guffra. They receive daily ration of high protein liquid food.

17. A Danakil woman scoops a kettleful of muddy water from a nearly dry hole in the bed of a river.

18. Supplies leaving Addis Ababa for SIM relief centers in the north. Words on tractor read, "Gift of the German Mission to the Blind."

19. Helimission of Switzerland donated the use of this helicopter for six weeks. Chief pilot Ernst Tanner directs unloading at Addis Ababa.

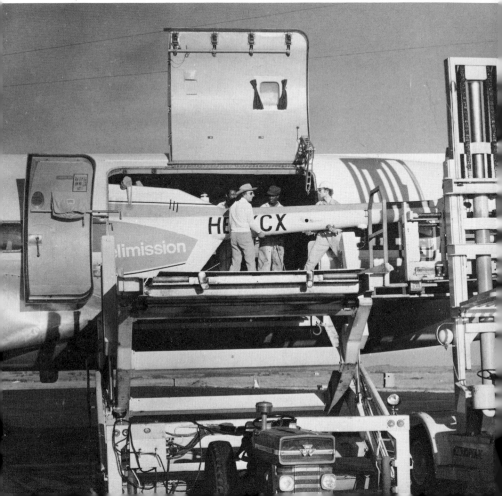

6. Crisis

The situation reached crisis proportions during late June, and became even worse during July and August. The north was in tragic turmoil as streams of famine victims flowed relentlessly into the towns along the road.

Relief centers were swamped even as they were being organized. SIM went all-out to do everything it could, as fast as it could. The Mission was not prepared for this kind of work. It had to improvise. It had to call on volunteers, and take missionaries away from other jobs. It asked other people in Ethiopia to help. Some people spent their vacation time helping. The churches responded immediately. Many young Ethiopians volunteered.

But during those summer months the pace was killing and the volume of human suffering devastating. Workers went to help for a week, or two weeks, or three weeks. There was a constant shuffle of personnel. Sometimes there was desperate understaffing.

SIM selected Dessie and Alamatta as their two relief bases. Dr. Schmoll was looking after things at Dessie, and Ken Radach headed north to organize Alamatta.

Alamatta is in north Wollo province, Dessie in south Wollo. South Wollo felt the impact a little sooner than north Wollo did. There were two mission houses at Alamatta. Ken and Gloria Radach moved into one of them.

They used the two-room schoolhouse as the relief building. The only other building, the clinic, had more than it could care for. Mary Amalia, with an Ethiopian dresser (paramedic), was looking after scores of sick people every day.

Supplies had been ordered. The first shipment of 25 tons of corn was on its way. Another 35 tons would follow from Asmara. Ken had to work fast. People were crowding around the station in increasing numbers every day, begging for food and medicine and shelter.

Ken had two immediate tasks. One was to erect a shelter for the unfortunate people, where they would at least be protected from the rain. His heart bled at the sight of the weak and sick lying on the wet ground. The other was to make a survey of the area around Alamatta, to find out, as best he could, how many people he had to deal with. He wanted to keep as many of them as possible in their villages, which would mean taking aid to them. He also wanted to know how big an influx Alamatta could expect as the situation worsened.

It was also immediately apparent that simply giving uncooked grain to many of the victims was useless. They couldn't tolerate it. It gave them diarrhea. The missionaries brewed huge pots of tea, sweetened with sugar, for those whose stomachs would not accept solids. Ken devised a scheme for baking injera and a coarse bread for those who could not eat grain.

He rounded up long eucalyptus poles and erected the framework for a huge shed. He roofed it with sheets of corrugated aluminum, and closed it in with more sheets. In no time it was filled with sick and hungry.

He made a smaller shed to store grain and supplies, set up a simple registration system, and took off with his son and a team of Ethiopian volunteers to survey the district.

They surveyed 33 villages close to Alamatta, making careful registrations of the ones in need, taking an inventory of each family's situation. The cards listed the number of men and women and children in each household, their ages, how many had died, how many were ill, what their illnesses appeared to be, whether or not the husband and father was home, how many animals were left... all the information he felt would be needed, not just for the present, but for future rehabilitation.

He and his helpers found that human nature was the same in northern Ethiopia as all over the world. There were those who openly tried to gain advantage of the situation. Attempts at cheating were common. Some large landowners tried to get the teams to list all their relatives, regardless of whether or not they were in need. For the most part, Ken and his partners were not fooled. The Ethiopian helpers knew their people well, knew the language better than Ken, and found it easier to detect deception.

The teams quickly learned to spot the most destitute. "We can tell where the hungry people are," Ken explained to them. "They've removed thatch from their houses to sell, there are no livestock around, the place in general looks rundown."

Such observations were not foolproof, though. Ken was tempted to bypass one house which was well kept, with a recently swept yard, and a thick crown of thatch. But he had decided that the team members should check every dwelling, regardless, so he approached the hut.

The door was slightly open. He pushed it open more, and let in enough light to reveal a woman, emaciated and haggard, lying on the floor. Beside her were two small bodies.

"I gave birth to these twins last night," she told Ken and Tazazu, his helper. She did not have to tell the rest of her story. She had been completely alone during the birth — a situation unheard of in that culture. The twins had died before morning. In any case, she had no strength of body to keep them alive. Her breasts were leathery and dry, her body wizened and shriveled like that of an old woman. But she was not old.

Tazazu called the neighbors and told them what had happened. The men agreed to bury the babies, and Ken and Tazazu lifted the weeping mother into their vehicle. They took her to the clinic at Alamatta, to be cared for there.

Ken was told that the attitude of many of the Muslim Galla tribespeople of the area had altered radically. The SIM station at Alamatta had been there for 19 years, with a somewhat checkered history of staffing because of the very small response. The Gallas were resentful of outsiders. They were arrogant and independent. They had been known to show their disdain for "foreigners," which included even bus passengers from Addis Ababa, by squatting in front of a bus in the middle of the road.

Now they did not obstruct the buses. Instead, helpless and hungry, they crowded around the buses when they stopped, begging the strangers for food or money. They welcomed Ken and his helpers, hoping that this would be the beginning of more help.

Despite their profession of Islam, most did not work hard at their religion. Mosques were few, and not many local people prayed, fasted, or went to Mecca. They were more animist than Muslim. Many Orthodox Christians lived among them also. The famine shattered the faith of many.

Ken found most local officials appreciative and cooperative. They studied his registration system and his distribution of food system, and adopted it for their use, too.

All during the survey and registration, Ken was working on ways to get food in to the villages. He knew beyond doubt that that was the only way to solve the problem of refugees. Aid had to go to them. They had to be kept at home, where they could live more normal lives, be active about their own affairs, and not as susceptible to contagious disease. He came to another conclusion: they would have to limit themselves to feeding the starving. There was no way they could help all who were hungry.

The sanitation and public health problems in the shelters that were being built along the great road were appalling. The shelters were just that — roofs with palm leaf mats for walls. As soon as they were completed, the people swarmed in, each person or family staking out an area for their own. Every inch of ground was taken. There was no space for walkways. The people had to step over each other to get in and out.

Water supply was often inadequate, and sanitation was virtually impossible. As in the streets of the towns, people urinated and defecated and vomited where they were, sometimes too weak to stand. But no one had had experience with this kind of emergency before. It took time to sort out the problems and devise solutions that really worked.

It was no wonder that cholera broke out. Contaminated food and drinking water carried the disease everywhere. When cholera struck, it killed in a matter of hours. Victims lost body fluid through excessive diarrhea, and lay helplessly weak wherever they happened to be.

The only way to save the victim's life was to replace lost body fluid. If the patient was too far gone to take fluid by mouth, it had to be given intravenously. But if given in time, it worked wonders. IV, as intravenous became known, was the only hope for many.

At Dessie, SIM nurse Chris Ott joined a group of government workers to form a cholera treatment team. At the village of Harbo there had been 300 deaths before the team got there to start treatment.

They took over a schoolhouse. Patients were placed on the floor and IV bags hung to nails in the wall. Drinking water was treated with halazone. Most of the victims recovered, and the epidemic was stopped, in that place at least.

A missionary of the Bible Churchmen's Missionary Society, Rhena Taylor, volunteered to help, and was sent to the government relief camp at Wurgeisa, north of Dessie, where Dr. Schmoll and Les Unruh had first seen the tragedy. Her experience was similar to all those who took part in the relief effort during that terrible crisis. This is how she reported it:

I am a desk-bound missionary, working with an office staff in Addis Ababa. I heard an appeal for funds, and felt frustrated that my missionary allowance didn't enable me to give significantly. But the appeal was also for personnel.

I read Matthew 25 carefully and the Lord spoke to me. I offered my services, making it abundantly clear that I was not a nurse, and hoping inwardly that nothing would happen. But SIM was in need. Two days after my offer I was being transported north to Wurgeisa.

The camp was a fenced-in enclosure with mud buildings with tin roofs. But the people were too many for the shelter and lay about the compound and around the doors of the camp. There were the old, muttering vaguely; mothers holding their emaciated babies toward me for help; children whose parents had died, sitting alone, weak and bewildered.

I had wondered what I could do. But work lay in front of me. When a woman, too feeble to go to the water, lies calling for a drink; when there are sores to be dressed, dirty bodies to be washed, clothes to be found, food to be given... I ended the day exhausted.

There was a house where the orphaned lived. Many were sick and weak, though others were growing stronger. The first night I was there, four died. I stood looking at the little bodies curled up on the mud floor, little claw-like hands extended for help, which, though offered, came too late.

I had wondered how I would react to death, but it became all too familiar. "Another five have died," would come the word. "Call the gravediggers." They would be taken out to the mass burial ground, where over 600 had been buried from that camp alone.

Thank God for those who were sending aid — the life-saving grain, the milk...

We lacked people. Nurses to save the dying, organizers who could see to the feeding program. It is no easy thing to feed 500 people. There is not time to coax the woman who is too weak to eat, or the child who does not care any longer.

Those who worked got ill. One of the young Ethiopian men helping us, the one who gave out the milk, went down with typhoid. In such a case, who notices that he is not there, and sees that the milk is given out? After the weary day, who goes to his house to treat him?

Water is not brought, and they cannot make the tea. The sugar is still in the storehouse, and the people are calling, "We are hungry... help my child... help me..."

People had no energy left to weep for the child of another. It seemed that no one cared except God in heaven, who surely looked down in loving pity on those who suffered. With His name on my lips I suffered with the suffering, knowing in my heart the truth of the words, "Blessed is he that considereth the poor..." (Psalm 41:1).

I rarely had time to look up and around me, though in fact the mountains there are beautiful. But once I did. I had stopped beside a woman because she was crying. The tears made dark channels down her dust-covered cheeks. It was a long time since I had seen someone cry in the camp. Most of us were beyond tears. Instead, there was a kind of dull, unresolved heartache that feared expression.

"What's the matter?" I asked — fatuous words in this place of starvation and death.

"My child is dead."

I looked down at what I should have seen in the first place, a tiny bundle of rags on the ground. I uncovered it. The child lay stiff, his hands crossed on his breast, his eyes closed. He was tiny, but I knew he could be several years old. Slow starvation does that to children.

I have not forgotten that moment. I knelt beside her and took her hand. We were an isolated group, she and I and that dead child. And I had nothing to say, nothing to ease the agony of bereaved motherhood in this bitter, fallen world. I could only let my heart hurt with hers, for the pity of it, for the waste of a child's life, for the whole, chaotic, desperate mess of famine and its aftermath.

But as I knelt, I looked up and saw a flight of birds wheeling through the air. Jesus' words flooded into my mind: "Are not two sparrows sold for a farthing? and one of them shall not fall on the ground without your Father.... Fear ye not therefore, ye are of more value..." (Matt. 10:29).

In the camp, grain was baked on open fires into thick pancake-type loaves; dry, unappetizing, almost impossible for the older ones, with rotting teeth and stomachs that had been feeding on grass, to eat, let alone digest. But there was milk, and a high-protein food for the children, and some water, and gradually we worked on getting better food.

But so many other things were not there. People were clothed in rags and there were no coverings even for those shaking in fever. We had no truck in which we could have visited the villages around.

We were short of every utensil... things to mix the milk in, to wash dishes in, to cook in. It was a constant battle to find firewood.

We had no soap with which we could have encouraged the people to wash and so prevent the skin-tearing disease of scabies. When we gave out milk we gave it to over 200 people in two tin mugs.

We were short of personnel. The workers were willing, but became sick so quickly. Ethiopian and foreigner alike fell victim to typhus, typhoid, and malaria. And all the time people were dying and the dead were left unmourned, untouched, save by the gravediggers who came each morning to take them to the mass grave, where hyenas fought and snarled as soon as darkness came.

Once five died in a night. With them lay a woman, feebly moving and unconscious, so near death that the gravediggers had bound her limbs as they had the others.

"No!" I said. "Don't take her! She is not dead!"

They looked indifferent. "What can you do for her?"

"Nothing. But she is not dead!"

"Well, let her be taken with the rest. We'll leave her at the side of the grave until she has died. It will save coming back for her."

"No!" I said again, my anger rising, a feeling of sick helplessness overcoming me. "She must stay here."

They left her to pacify me, but an hour later I saw she had been taken.

There have been those who, standing in the midst of such scenes, have raised clenched fists and cursed the Creator for allowing such misery, such suffering, such waste of life. I could not do that. The God I had known throughout my youth, and now, had not changed to being an uncaring overlord. He had created man in His own image to enjoy the things of the earth, to be fruitful and multiply. If man had chosen his own way, if the earth had been abused, and made waste, this was not God's fault.

If my eyes wept at this sight, so more did His who taught me compassion. If I was crushed, bowed down at the weight of death and sickness, at seeing bodies tormented with hunger and thirst, was He not also suffering?

Ken was aware of the problems of the shelters, and tried hard to keep them to a minimum at Alamatta, and, more important, prevent them from happening, by keeping the people in their villages. He was to achieve a great measure of success in that, because around Alamatta the villages were more accessible than in some areas. There were roads and paths, and transport into the villages was easier — if not easy — than in some other parts of the north.

He went into action immediately, with the survey results in hand, to move grain and food and medicine into the 33 villages clustered around the town. But there was nothing he could do for the more distant villages. During July and August, the effects of famine drew people from farther and farther afield. By the end of July SIM's center at Alamatta was providing food for 3000 people, in addition to supplying 3500 people in the villages.

A food preparation called Fafa came to the rescue of thousands of victims. It was a soft porridge, easily prepared, made of soybean meal, milk powder, sugar, and other grain. It was cooked in clay pots. The Government set up places to manufacture it and distributed it widely. Babies, the aged, and those in advanced conditions of starvation could eat it easily and digest it readily. Ken set up a special Fafa camp at Alamatta.

During July and August, Mary Amalia was a key figure in Alamatta. A Canadian, Mary was not a nurse, but had had 11 years' experience with SIM in Somalia and Ethiopia. She was not fluent in Amharic, the main Ethiopian language, because most of her years had been spent in Somalia. But she readily went to Alamatta to help out. She was given clinic responsibilities, aided by very capable Christian Ethiopian dressers.

Many families coming from areas far from the main road were separated. In one case, not knowing where to find help, the father of a family took the two boys and went in one direction, the mother took the two girls and went another.

The mother found her way to Alamatta, after burying one little girl on the way. Mary did her best, but the woman was too weak, and died. That had been a very busy day, and in the afternoon Mary could find no one to do the simple preparation of the bodies of those who had died that day, and dig the common grave.

She enlisted some young boys, put on her smock, and went to work herself. She wrapped the body of the woman in a piece of cloth. As she worked, a man came up and asked for work. She readily offered him food if he would help dig the grave. She showed him the bodies, gave him instructions, and left.

In a few minutes he came running to Mary in great anguish. "It is my wife!" he cried, as he fell at Mary's feet and through his tears kissed her feet. "Thank you for taking care of her. I was afraid she had died on the road, with no one to bury her. The hyenas might have eaten her. Thank you!"

Mary could not hold back the tears. "This is the mercy of God," the man said. "I will have the joy of burying her myself. May God reward you!"

He hugged his daughter to him as he made ready for the burial. Then Mary learned that he had buried both his sons, too, along the road. He stayed and worked at the shelter for some time, with a grateful heart.

In mid-August, Don Stilwell organized a relief caravan in Addis Ababa and set out for the north. At Dessie they stopped to pick up Chris Ott, the smiling German nurse who had been on the cholera IV team. She would go with them to Alamatta and take over from Mary.

There were three vehicles and a trailer, carrying food, medicine, Fafa, IV solution, powdered milk, and other supplies. The first stop was Wurgeisa. Town officials were working hard at providing improved shelters, and Zelleke, an SIM public health supervisor, had arrived the day previous to set up a rehydration center. Cholera was still prevalent in many areas, and Wurgeisa was providing emergency treatment for many victims.

Chris found the situation critical, and got to work immediately. "The people in the terminal stages of starvation were housed in a crude building nearby," she said. "We found the floor covered with people in the most pitiable condition. There were 50 of them in a room measuring about 15 feet square.

"The two young men had no car with which to bring people to the shelter. They carried the dying from the roadside. They were ill with diarrhea, and hardly any flesh remained on their bones. We brought them into a schoolroom and started them on IV. Some of the IV bags were hung from nails in the wall, others were simply held by people who wanted to help. I got 10 IV's going in an hour."

Chris could see that a woman in the middle of the floor had died. Her baby was lying beside her. There was also a young girl who still had some life in her. "Give the baby a drink every half hour," Chris ordered the girl. The girl looked blank. Chris wondered if she knew what a half hour was.

Outside the crowded shelter a girl was sitting, holding a wasted baby whose mother had just died. "What shall I do?" the girl implored Chris. What could anybody do? Sitting there also was a little boy about three years old. Chris gave him a bun, which he began devouring. He had been brought back from the grave yesterday, when he was about to be buried with his mother. The gravediggers thought he was dead, too, until someone saw him move slightly. He was given IV fluids, and responded. "When I saw him sitting there eating the bun," Chris said, "I could hardly restrain the tears."

About 300 refugees were gathered in orderly fashion, awaiting their portion of food, some receiving cooked whole grain, some Fafa, and some flour, which they would cook themselves.

They moved on to the town of Mersa, arriving just after dark. Conditions there were even worse. There were about 1000 people sitting in lines on both sides of the road, unable to get into the shelter that the government had erected.

They decided to spend the night. The local governor was eager for their help, and insisted on showing them the camp by lamplight.

There was a rather satisfactory rain shelter, where several hundred of the "healthy hungry" were housed. They were given rations of whole wheat, which they boiled or roasted, although for many of them it was completely indigestible. Before the rain shelter had been built, 40 to 50 people had been dying daily. With the shelter, about 15 to 20.

In a second, smaller shelter, in which the mud walls were not yet dry, and the floor still wet, were people sick with "every disease one could think of." No mats covered the floor. People coughed and spat and gasped for breath.

That was not all. "They had a smaller house that was packed with about 40 people," Chris observed. "These were almost dead from starvation. They might have been brought back from the gates of death, but there was nobody to help them. It could have been labeled 'death house,' because every day they carried bodies from it to the grave."

It had been an exhausting day for nurse Chris. And she hadn't even reached Alamatta, the place of her appointment. But she could not refuse help to sufferers at her feet. "What could I do?" she said. "There in front of me was a woman crouched over her husband, who was breathing his last. The woman cried softly. In normal times she would have screamed as she saw her husband slipping away. There was no strength left for screaming."

Close by, another tragedy was being enacted. A small boy was leaning over the body of his dead father crying, "Father! Give me food! Give me water!" Chris gave him some boiled grain. "Here," she said. "Eat this." He looked at her helplessly. "How can I eat it dry?" he asked. "I have no water."

"There was no water, no medication, for this crowd of dying people," Chris declared. Don Stilwell decided that he would have to find somebody to come to Mersa and lend a hand. But who? Don thought about Mary Amalia.

Next day Chris joined the staff at Alamatta, and Mary agreed to go to Mersa. Chris did not have time to "settle in." She threw her sleeping bag on the floor, and started in. Over 300 people were sitting outside the gate, thin skeletons. Chris identified cases of cholera among them. She had them laid along the fence and under trees, and went down the line starting them on IV infusions.

She needed capable help, and with Mary leaving, Chris was relying on the senior Ethiopian dresser. But he, as other relief workers experienced, had reached the breaking point. The constant pressure of suffering, of death, of spiritual and emotional and physical anguish, added to the demands of long hours and constant toil, took its toll. "I must leave," he told her. "I can stand it no longer."

Emotional fatigue was a very real factor that relief workers and administrators had to recognize. One can only stand so much. If one doesn't get away from it, one breaks.

So Chris faced a 24-hour schedule. "The 24-hour part wasn't the only thing," Chris said. "There were no electric lights. We carried pressure lanterns with us at night. The water system had broken down, and we used chocolate brown water, carried from the river by local women. Cholera came with it. We had 260 cholera cases in 20 days. One day I gave 78 IV's. I was up night after night. After a week, I was about finished. I don't know what I would have done without the tremendous help of the Ethiopian dressers and others. They were marvelous."

With such conditions, it seemed that SIM and the many other relief agencies that were coming to the rescue were fighting a losing battle. In a sense, they were. There was the gnawing realization that somebody, somewhere, for some unknown reason, had started relief work too late.

But lives *were* being saved, and order was beginning to emerge from chaos.

7. The shelter

When Ali awoke, he was lying on a palm leaf mat with a blanket wrapped around him. His first thought was that he had been buried. He soon discovered that he was on top of the ground, and that there were people around him. The figure lying near him proved to be his wife.

Ali noticed a slight pain in his arm. He reached his right hand to the sore spot to investigate. A strangely dressed man restrained him. He explained to Ali that this was something to make him strong again. It was medicine.

Then Ali understood. He asked the question, just to be sure. Yes, the man told him, this was the shelter. Yes, there was food.

"How did I get here?" Ali asked.

A truck had come along the road, he was told. It was the shelter truck, driven by Ken Radach. He and his two Ethiopian assistants had seen the family lying unconscious by the roadside. They put them in the back of the truck, on blankets, and brought them in. There had not been room inside the shelter, so they were outside, but the medicine was saving their lives.

The man moved on. Ali looked around him some more. The medicine thing was attached to his arm somehow, and a cord of a kind he had not seen before ran from it to the top of a fence post. There was another strange device, with what seemed to be water in it. The man who had spoken to him, and others like him, walked up and down the fence, touching the water containers and looking at the people on the ground.

He tried to understand this new, upside down world. He realized that he felt stronger. He began to think of different kinds of magic he had seen practiced in his town and in the market. This was real magic. It worked. Had he been told that he was being fed through his arm, he would not have believed it. There is no other way to be fed, he knew, than through the mouth.

There were 70 other patients lying along the fence, although Ali could see only those next to him. He was glad that Maryam was there. What about the children? He would ask the man, if he came back. But right now, Ali was exhausted. The turn of events was too much to comprehend. He went back to sleep.

Both Ali and his wife lay on the ground receiving food intravenously for 24 hours. They asked about the children, and were told that his three sons were fine and getting stronger. But the little three-year-old daughter had been too tired. Her life had gone. The men had buried her close by. This was hard for Ali and Maryam to accept.

On the morning of the second day, they could stand up and move around among the people. As a family they found a place to sit, and were grateful for returning strength and for food to eat.

They were finally led to the shelter, bewildered by the hundreds of people — bent, gaunt, hollow-eyed men, women, and children. Most were sitting quietly, with a minimum of personal belongings around them: a tin can, a few clothes, a walking stick. Each was grateful for the least token of human care. Out there was starvation. Within the camp there was food, love, and concern.

Ali and Maryam were very happy to be with their boys. They were becoming acquainted with the others around them. It seemed to them that hardly a family in the shelter was intact.

There were dozens of children without parents. They had been cast on their own in the midst of the famine, and had made their way to the shelter.

But the family's rejoicing at being alive gradually gave way to boredom. The boys played some games with other children, but they also got into some fights with them. One thing they loved was to learn songs from workers who taught them to the group. The songs were mostly about Yesus, someone quite unknown to the boys.

There was much talk about Yesus, Ali learned. As a Muslim, he had heard the name, but Ali knew very little about Islam, and less about its teachings and its prophets. Yesus, however, he concluded, must be worth knowing about.

After the morning meal each day, he looked forward to the words from the preacher, as well as to the visit from the white-clad nurses and their assistants, with their medicines and questions. Most evenings were spent hearing Bible stories, and learning more songs about Yesus.

When Ali asked if he could have work, he was told to help with digging the daily grave. It was a sad task, but it needed doing, and Ali was grateful that it was he who was digging. Maryam was asked to help sift and clean the grain before it was ground for cooking. They were grateful to have a part in the life of the shelter that had helped them.

They were not sure what to think when they were told that their boys could attend the shelter's school. The boys were excited yet timid when told about it. With a little encouragement, they entered, and soon found that paper could talk.

There was no school in Ali and Maryam's village. They had never learned to read and write. They felt no particular need to learn, and in any case, there was no one to teach them. On those rare occasions when a paper had to be signed by Ali, he did as his neighbors did, and affixed his thumb print, hoping that what the paper said was true.

Now his sons were learning to read, and to write. They were also learning verses from the Christian's Holy Book — truths about God, His Son, and His love. Increasingly their hearts were opening to believe the message they heard, of eternal life and forgiveness through the sacrifice of Yesus, the Holy One.

Each evening they came together to share the events of the day, and to talk about their future. For with the return of life, came the realization that there would be tomorrows. And tomorrows needed planning. Their great hope was to go home.

But going home was not a simple thing. There was nothing at home. There was no food. The oxen were dead. The animals were dead. The house would be the worse for neglect. The fields would have to be plowed. There was no seed grain. There was still no promise of rain.

It was a big problem. Ali did not have the answer.

8. Miss Mary

The day after Chris Ott arrived at Alamatta, Ken Radach drove Mary Amalia down to the government shelter at Mersa. The Land-Rover was loaded with all the supplies he could muster.

In the town there was a motel of sorts, where he arranged accommodation and meals for Mary. Then he introduced her to Zeleka, the Ethiopian public health worker who was in charge of the 50 SIM leprosy control centers in Wollo province, and who had also gone to Mersa to help out.

Then they went to the camp. Mary described the situation in this report:

Do you know what a pine forest looks like after a fire has gone through? Burnt-out gray logs, fallen and dry? The people were lying all over each other like dry, gray, fallen trees.

Children with swollen faces and swollen tummies were there, suffering with edema from malnutrition; grown people also, just lying, fallen, hopeless. I heard that about 35 had been buried that day.

I froze. "God, whatever will I do? I felt you wanted me to come here, but what *can* I do? Oh, Lord, give me strength and wisdom!"

As I stood there looking and wondering, along came the Governor of Wollo Province, with the local administrator and other officials. They shook hands with me (I was wearing my Ethiopian dress and shawl) and warmly welcomed me. I was introduced to the Ethiopian representative of the Community Development Department, who had been trying to do something but had found the job overwhelming.

Their first question was, "What is your program for the shelter?"

I had some ideas from my work at Alamatta. The greatest need I could see was for fluids for the badly dehydrated people. I could look over the crowd and see those to whom I would give IV right away. I said my program would be to get liquid and protein nourishment to the starving, and medicine to the sick, and to organize the camp.

"What do you need right now, to get started?"

I had just been into the shelter for the most desperately ill. People had vomited on the dirt floor, and because they could not move they had excreted there also. The flies and filth and stench were appalling. I felt I just couldn't walk among them.

So I said, "My first job is to clean up this house. Please will you help me get some brooms?"

"There are no brooms in town," the local administrator said.

"What can I use?"

"We use branches from trees."

"Well, can you please have somebody get me some branches?"

They called for volunteers and some men went off for branches. I asked if the patients could be carried outside while we cleaned the house. They helped in this, too.

When the branches arrived, nobody wanted to sweep, so I rolled up my sleeves, put my shawl over my shoulders and set to work. When the men saw me, they grabbed branches, too, and all of them helped me sweep.

Sheets of corrugated iron and some shovels appeared from somewhere. The men piled the dirt on the sheets and carried it away. The distinguished visitors wouldn't quit.

"What do you want now?" they asked.

"Sand, to put on the floor," I replied.

Within an hour they had seen that enough sand was brought from the dry bed of the nearby river to cover the floor. I had the patients brought back in, placing the worst cases on the floor by the walls. I asked for big nails and we pounded them into the walls, and hung IV bags from them.

The officials thanked me warmly, encouraged me, and said they would be back the next day. They asked again what I wanted. I said I was frustrated because I couldn't talk to the people. I needed an interpreter, someone who would really stick with me.

A group of young people had been following us around. One

stepped up, spoke to me in English, said his name was Aaragow, and offered to work with me. I asked him what grade he was in at school.

"Eleventh grade," he said. School was not in session, so he could help.

I liked his looks. He was bright and intelligent. So I said, "All right, you will be my mouth."

And he was, for the next two weeks of my stay. He was right there with me the whole time.

After the men had gone, I turned to Aaragow and the Community Development man, and said, "We're going to see how much we can get organized here before those men come back tomorrow."

We worked late, giving IV's, having water hauled from the hole in the river bed, and purifying it with halazone. I made electrolyte solution, to replace needed chemicals in dehydrated bodies, and we encouraged as many people as we could to drink it.

Next morning we were up about 5:15. I told my helpers we would start each day with Bible reading and prayer. The Lord was our strength and help. We were overjoyed to find that only four people out of that great mass had died during the night.

That day an Ethiopian high school girl, Gaiti, arrived from Alamatta to help me. She was tremendous — a hard worker, cheerful in the midst of pressure, and with a bright Christian testimony. She was about 18. She was a real joy to me.

By noon the next day, I had the cooking area set up and water boiled over open fires for the porridge. I had asked for and received five metal drums, and had a local blacksmith cut them in half. The Community Development man had come up with dishes and drinking glasses.

I called for volunteers and appointed one to be in charge of the Fafa porridge, one to mix and pour the electrolyte solution, another to mix the milk powder, and another to make tea.

The Town Administrator was around continually asking, "What do you need? How can I help?" On request he brought a large sack of salt, another of sugar, plus wood for the fire, as well as tea.

I had my sleeves rolled up again and had a wooden paddle in my hands stirring porridge when the officials returned. They had hardly been able to find me because of the crowd watching the food cooking. They thanked me profusely and remarked about the changes they could see already.

They could hardly believe that only four people had died that night.

One of the needs was to get despondent, immobile patients on their feet again. This took strong talk, especially for those inside the sick house. So I made a line on the ground a short distance from the building and told them they all had to walk that far before they would get more food. Some of them cried and said it was impossible.

"Those who can, get up and walk!" I ordered. "You who want to help, lift these others to their feet and put their arms around your shoulders. Help them walk to that line!" And they did.

The work went on day after day, from early in the morning until late at night. We soon had 1052 patients receiving daily treatment. Our staff grew with the arrival of another medical dresser and two evangelists from churches in southern Ethiopia.

Zeleka had a long shed built to get the people out of the heat of the day and the cold of the night. The Red Cross sent funds and supplies. Other help arrived from both Ethiopian and foreign sources.

To keep up morale, I used to joke with the people, and mimic the way they limped around. They loved it. Then Gaiti started singing and teaching gospel songs to the patients. The people got stronger as they sang.

I'll never forget waking up one night after a long day, and hearing a lot of noise at the camp. I sat up and listened. I heard them singing at the top of their voices, in Amharic:

Thank you, thank you, Jesus.
Thank you, Jesus, in my heart.

Love you, love you, Jesus.
Love you, Jesus, in my heart.

I can't live without you.
I can't live without you in my heart.

Tears came to my eyes, and I repeated the same thing — in *my* heart.

Later we got palm mats for the sick to lie on, and eventually had them for all the people. We had a routine each morning. The patients rolled up their mats and carried them outside while they swept the house and the whole camp.

But I had times of depression. The weariness got me down. I began to brood over my lack of medical knowledge. And yet day by day the Lord gave me wisdom in diagnosis and treatment, so that almost all the patients recovered.

One night I was so tired I couldn't eat, and when Gaiti tried to get me to eat, I told her I had to meet the Lord first.

"Lord," I asked, "are you satisfied with me? I'm not satisfied with myself, and I just can't manage all these difficult cases."

Almost immediately He gave me His answer through I Corinthians 1:27 — "But God hath chosen the foolish things of the world to confound the wise; and God hath chosen the weak things of the world to confound the things which are mighty."

I said, "Thank you, Lord. That's me. And I thank you that you chose me and want to use me. And I *am* willing. Just help me to carry on."

Then I was able to eat.

The death rate held between four and six each day. That was remarkable. The hardest thing, though, was to treat people and do everything in the middle of a crowd. It was especially hard to deliver babies, with no privacy and nothing sterile.

One afternoon I was called to help a woman who was in labor. The woman and I were crowded by a wall of people watching every move. I arrived just as the child was born. It was a small, but healthy-looking boy. I was kneeling on the ground, trying to care for the new baby and clean up the mother, when the District Governor appeared! I couldn't shake hands, as is almost mandatory when such an official appears, so I gave him my elbow and a smile.

He stood right there and made a little speech.

"I just came to thank you," he began. "You have been doing so very much for my people. I can see that you really love them. I have seen you cry with the mothers whose children have died. And I've seen you carry a patient in your arms, your skirt and your feet filthy with his waste. And now with this new baby... I want to thank you for helping my people so much."

I took the opportunity right then to tell him through Aaragow where that love came from. "I believe God sent me here to help you. If you see love for your people in me, it is His love. I love your people and I want to help them, but it is God who is helping you through me. He wants you to know Him and love Him, and to receive His gift of love, Jesus Christ, the Savior."

The Governor was very quiet. He nodded his head, with all eyes watching him, and again he said, "Thank you. I came because I want to thank you again for all you are doing." The people murmured their assent.

One day during my early morning devotions, I was reading Psalm 125:2. When the staff met for devotions I shared it with them. "As the mountains are round about Jerusalem, so the Lord is round about his people from henceforth even for ever."

I asked the staff members to put "Mersa" in place of "Jerusalem." We looked at the ranges of mountains around us and thanked the Lord that He was surrounding us, helping us, as His children, to serve those in the camp with love. The load was increasing, for hungry people were still coming in and crying for help.

The day wore on with importunate people always at my elbow. Then there was a call to help in another delivery. This time it was premature twins and a very weak mother. When the first baby was born dead, a cry of deep sympathy went all through the watching crowd.

Then the second tiny baby was born. But the placenta was retained. For some reason, I broke down, crying. I felt sorry for myself, and asked again, "Why isn't there a real midwife here to handle this?"

I was at the end of myself, and I feared for the life of the mother. Gaiti and Aaragow wept with me, and then Gaiti spoke up. "Miss Mary, didn't you read to us this morning that the Lord was here with us to help us? Let's pray and ask Him to help."

We prayed, and ten minutes later the placenta came normally. The baby was small and had no chance to survive in that kind of situation. It died in the morning, but the mother lived. I was grateful for that.

After about two weeks of this I was completely worn out. I was grateful when word came that the Red Cross would probably take over the shelter. It was getting beyond our ability to handle the great crowds of people.

More relief organizations were coming into the country, and the government had set up a special Relief and Rehabilitation Commission, which places such groups in the most needy sectors.

Shortly after, Mary turned over the shelter to Red Cross workers and made her way to Addis Ababa for a well-deserved rest.

But many who were in Mersa in those days will not forget Miss Mary.

9. Hope

By September, Don Stilwell and his teams were beginning to see daylight. The picture was still desperately dark, in terms of human suffering, and the daylight was just a glimmer, like a bright glow at the far end of a long tunnel.

But things were beginning to shape up, with supply systems functioning better, and funds starting to come in, and assistance from government and other volunteer relief agencies absorbing more and more of the pressures.

The shelters continued to receive more people, and the scale of the work increased, but there was not quite the same desperate confusion that had reigned during the terrible weeks of July and August.

SIM workers now knew what to do, even if they didn't have the facilities to do it with. The picture was clearer concerning immediate needs, and what to expect following the peak, which was expected to come late in September, when some crops would be harvested by those who still farmed, and thus ease the pressure a little.

The world was alerted to the situation by this time, and knew of the tragedy that was affecting so many people right across Africa, not only in Ethiopia. Volunteers began to arrive from many countries. Money began to come in. Relief agencies moved in and began to help.

The situation was not one that could be quickly cared for. Even if adequate relief centers were established, and steady supplies of food and medicine flowing, and systems functioning to keep hungry people fed and housed, the problem would not be solved. Tens of thousands of people cannot stay indefinitely in relief camps. Governments cannot feed hundreds of thousands of people, even in their villages, indefinitely. Health problems, bad enough in the best of times, were becoming horrendous in scope.

There would have to be a mopping-up operation, after things were well in hand, and after that ten thousand things would have to be done to put things back to normal. And beyond that, tedious and expensive though it would be, was the necessity to break the common pattern of the past century, and introduce patterns that would prevent as much as possible the recurrence of such suffering.

Don Stilwell and Ken Radach and Dr. Schmoll and the many people who worked with them realized that their task was just beginning. And during the emergency conditions that surrounded them, they began to work slowly toward the greater end.

With the help of the volunteers who arrived at Alamatta, some for just a couple of weeks, others for longer, Ken saw the SIM center grow into a major base. The main shelter became a sturdy building 120 feet long and 45 feet wide, properly roofed and walled.

The system of food distribution at the shelter worked well, and although the place was crowded to the fence, it functioned efficiently.

There were some happy incidents taking place now, as well as the tragedies. Chris Ott was encouraged by one woman who joined her, baby on her back, as she walked back to the camp after treating a sick patient.

"She thanked me for the help she had received," Chris said. "She told me, 'With God's help you have given me back my baby, who was dying. With the medicine, and the Fafa, she is better now. Tomorrow we are going home after we receive our supply of grain.'

"There was a new swing in her step, and hope written on her face. Her 12-year-old girl gladly held the goatskin bag open for the supply of grain allotted to the small family, and then the group of four, for there was also a skinny little six-year-old boy in a torn shirt with them, was ready to head for home."

One little eight-year-old boy had walked for two days without food, alone, on the point of starvation, to the shelter. His name was Desalem, meaning "the world's joy." His mother had died, and his father could not be found. Probably he had died, too. Desalem arrived at a very bad time, at night, when all the food in the feeding program had been eaten. More was expected the next day, but every scrap was gone.

The missionaries fed him, and five others, with their own food. He had nothing but a sack to cover him at night, so they put him in the injera house to sleep, where it was warm.

The next day he was told to sit in the sun, to keep warm and dry, but he said, "No, I'd rather work for you." Betty Braithwaite let him help here and there, and made sure he had food.

"He always looked puzzled when I prayed before he ate," Betty said. "After a preaching service one day he came to me with a black string around his neck, an Orthodox custom, as evidence that he wanted to be a Christian. It was the only thing he knew about Christianity, having come from an Islamic background."

Betty explained the good news of the gospel to him, and he seemed to understand. He touched her heartstrings one evening when he was given some bread, and Betty smiled at him and said pleasantly, "Oh, that looks good." Desalem looked up solemnly and brought it to her. He laid it in her lap as his gift to her.

Another remarkable event occurred when a boy about 16 years old was carried in to the shelter. He was unconscious, and no one had any hope that he would survive. He was given an IV infusion, and clung to life. He was given another. In all, he received 12 infusions, and eventually responded.

He was nicknamed "Twelve IV" and spent some time in the camp. He listened very intently to the gospel message as it was explained daily. One day he was talking with Betty Braithwaite.

She said to him, "God has spared you for a purpose, do you realize that?"

"Yes," he replied, "I've received my life back all right, I know that!"

Betty explained to him again the way of salvation, and encouraged him to attend the church service next day. He did, and took a stand for Christ. He went to Betty with a beaming face every day the next week, wanting to help in any way he could.

The sequel to his story, later that year, was that he was among the first group to be baptized at Alamatta, and became one of the members of the new church that started there.

Ken was having good success in the villages for which SIM was responsible around Alamatta, which grew in number to about 50. Grain was taken by truck to the little communities, and enough grain supplied to each family to keep them in food for three weeks at a time. Ken's registration system made this possible, with allotments apportioned for each member, child or adult, and the head of the household made responsible for receiving and acknowledging the food.

In some villages of the area, as throughout the north, the people seemed reasonably prosperous. They had cows, sheep, goats, and chickens. "Even these have a rough time feeding themselves," Ken reported, "but they are not destitute."

They felt sorry for all who were having a struggle, but they knew their limitations, and kept to their policy of caring only for those who were in critical need, not for all who were hungry.

In some areas the children roamed the fields collecting weeds and grass seed, which they cooked and ate. The drought had affected even weeds and grass, though. The ground was brown and hard and dry.

Ken also encouraged people in the camp to go back to their villages, once a supply route had been opened. Supply routes were a problem almost everywhere in the north. There were not many feeder roads leading into the villages from the towns along the great road. Some places had more than others, but all of them were narrow dirt roads, some of them not more than tracks.

A food-for-work program was started, in cooperation with government, to make new roads and improve poor ones. The men of the area put in their day's work right near home, and were paid on the spot in grain for their families. The people soon realized that they could return to their homes and still be fed.

Ken visited some of the villages that had been completely deserted a few weeks previously. The thatch was gone from many of the huts, and they looked derelict, but inside were family groups.

"We had gone to Alamatta to beg," an old woman told him. "Then we heard we could get grain in our own village, so we returned." Ken counted 25 families that had returned, some of them straggling in while he was there. "They were soon busy puttering around and straightening out their huts," he said. "They were happy to be home."

In the relief camps, the complexity of the disaster was becoming more and more apparent. One of the issues was the large number of orphans. Caring for them would have to be the primary responsibility of government, and a start was made to that end. Orphanages in the form of separate quarters were set up here and there. At Alamatta, one was established temporarily in the community center, which was a big barnlike structure that had once been a cotton factory. About 300 orphans slept there, with another 200 or so adults.

Chris Ott was concerned about these little ones who had lost their parents. "We are sending medical help and baby food and milk to support the effort of the government to care for these destitute children," she reported. "One of them is Desalem. I saw him again today. He is still emaciated, and his little face is so sad, even though he has had a wash and looks so smart in some clean clothing we had given him. But he still looks scared — he has forgotten how to smile."

The tragedy of the children was hard to take. So many had suffered starvation. In some cases, driven by utter desperation, mothers resorted to starving one child in order to keep the stronger ones alive. The effects of starvation were pathetic. Orphans sat expressionlessly, big eyes staring, but making not a sound. Babies opened their mouths to cry but had no strength.

"I have never seen such a concentration of immense human suffering," Chris Ott wrote. "Our hearts go out to all these whose lives spell nothing but sorrow and desperation. Day by day we look into these brown, haggard faces, and yet they brighten up when we are able to give them food and medicine. Their eyes respond even when we give them a smile. How wonderful that people at home are filling our hands so we can help them!"

Another problem concerned communicable diseases, some of which would have long-term effects, and would need long-term programs of treatment. Starvation creates low resistance, and even causes irreversible damage. In young children, particularly, mental ability can be adversely affected because of damage to brain and nerve tissue. The next generation of school-children will contain large numbers of slow learners because of the effects of starvation.

TB was readily observed as being a major disease.

"TB is our major concern," said one doctor in the north. "More people die from it than from any other disease. There must be a massive campaign of preventive treatment."

Staff at the Alamatta clinic reckoned that about 75 percent of the people who came for help were infected with it. One part of the shelter was set aside as their "Ward." But treatment for TB is long and tedious. For people who have no knowledge of the hygiene that is necessary to restore a patient, and just as necessary to prevent the spread of the disease, prescribing adequate remedy seemed hopeless.

TB was just another of the problems for which solutions would have to be found in the months and years that lay ahead.

The plight of the famine victims and the enormity of the disaster was now realized. Everyone, including the government, was working day and night to correct the situation.

For the government, however, it was too late. No one knew it at the time, but the famine was the factor that would soon discredit the government, and in a few months topple the throne. Some time in September, when the crisis was so bad, an independent British film crew headed by Jonathan Dimbleby went to Ethiopia to report. The film they made, mostly around Dessie, was later shown to the world on TV. It became a major tool in overthrowing the government.

10. Tigre

Tigre province lies next to Wollo, on the north. Dessie and Alamatta are in Wollo. Mai Chau is in Tigre. It is not many miles from Alamatta north to Mai Chau, and the countryside is not all that different, but when drought and famine struck the north, conditions in Tigre were not the same as in Wollo.

The drought was as severe, and as many people were affected, but Tigre was better prepared. The Governor had recognized the possibility of famine coming, especially after the rains had been poor for two years. He had stored grain and laid plans to get it out to the distressed areas if necessary.

He had personally supervised the building of feeder roads up and down the mountains, which made it possible to reach most towns and villages by vehicle. He had also laid out airstrips in strategic areas, so the province could be serviced by plane.

As a result, when hunger came, it was not necessary for large shelters to be built. The masses did not flee their villages looking for help. Some did, of course, but not on the scale that happened in Wollo.

When reports from outlying districts in mid-August made it apparent that grain distribution would have to get under way, the Governor asked George Middleton for assistance. George was Superintendent of SIM work in the north.

The Governor's request, specifically, was for help in getting food to the Danakil people. The Danakils are a nomadic or seminomadic tribe, tough, independent, proud Muslims, who live in the vast lowlands that stretch away to the east, reaching all the way to the Red Sea.

To reach them, one leaves the high mountainous escarpment through which the great road winds, and descends with breathtaking abruptness from the 8000 foot altitude of Makalle, the capital of Tigre province, to the treeless fields and hot, flat sands of the desert. Here, too, lies the great Danakil Depression, a huge bowl of scorching hot territory that in some places is below sea level.

The Danakils there move back and forth along the dry river courses, among scrub thorn bush, with their camels, sheep, goats, and cattle. They live in seemingly constant search of pasture and water, growing very little of anything, least of all, grain. What they need, they buy from the highland markets, with money obtained from the sale of their animals.

The Danakils live on the border of disaster even at the best of times. The drought had reduced them to desperate straits. They were starving, and the Governor intended to get food to them.

There was an enigma to the situation, an enigma that plagued relief work throughout the months of July, August, and September. These are the rainy season months. And although there had not been enough rain in preceding months and years to bring good crops, there was frequent rain during this season.

It was useless rain, for the most part, in terms of farming. It was a major hindrance and a cause of despair in terms of transportation. The sudden torrential downpours had their usual effect. The ground, though parched, could not absorb it rapidly enough. The soil became saturated on top, and the excess ran down every slope and gully. Dirt and gravel roads became morasses of sticky, heavy mud. Stream beds filled immediately and poured floods of water down their courses, making it impossible to ford them.

The Danakils could not drive their cattle to the highlands because of the rain-filled rivers. Vehicles could not negotiate the roads to the Danakil area. The only solution was to help them by air. But where could the planes land? There were very few places that merited airstrips, and so the decision was made to drop the grain from the air

The Governor would supply the grain — 50 tons of it. George was to plan and execute the operation. First he went to the Air Force base in Asmara. He told of the crisis in the Danakil area, but regulations made it impossible for them to provide aircraft.

George then went to the state airlines, Ethiopian Airlines, and chartered a DC3 cargo plane. These are considered the workhorses of Ethiopian Airlines, which uses them with great success in its rugged mountain flying. The Airlines offered a reduced rate, and Shell Oil donated the fuel, in light of the nature of the charter. SIM provided the funds.

The Governor accompanied George on the flights, which totalled 14. The grain was dropped near many settlements, most of them clusters of skin-covered portable structures shaped like beehives.

The airdrops undoubtedly saved the lives of several thousand people, although reports from such an inaccessible area were slow in coming out. And the Danakils were not a communicative people. There was no love lost between them and some of the other tribes. Their warlike raids of the past, which still cropped up on occasion, had established a backlog of hostility. Relations between the Danakils and the highland people were not always pleasant.

Later on, it was to be learned that the airdrops had had a remarkable effect on the Danakils who benefited by them, and led to a completely new and receptive attitude toward the missionaries.

The Governor was impressed with SIM cooperation and effort, and made a special request. Could SIM do a survey of the Danakil area of Tigre, with special attention to the medical needs? There would be no restrictions, and no objections if the Mission presented the gospel while the survey was done.

George agreed, and got in touch with Don Stilwell.

"We'll see if the Barlows can go," Don said. He picked up the phone and asked for the SIM hospital at Dilla, about 200 miles south of Addis Ababa. Dr. Nathan Barlow and his wife, Doris, had served in Ethiopia with SIM since 1945. Their work had been mostly in the southern provinces, where Nathan had become a living legend among the Wallamo and Darassa people. He had played a major role in public health work, and had been a key figure in identifying and stemming more than one major epidemic.

He and Doris were indefatigable. They were at ease anywhere in Ethiopia, under any conditions. They had roamed the south on medical assignments many times. They knew how to rough it. With Doris at his side, Nathan, it seemed, could handle almost anything.

Within a few days the Barlows had begun a three-week survey trip of the Danakil area east of Makalle. Despite the poor condition of the roads, they were taken to their first survey base, Debub, by Land-Rover. This is a light, four-wheel drive vehicle designed for rugged travel. George Middleton drove them in, with an Ethiopian assistant for Nathan, and saw them set up in camp before leaving.

The next few days, with generous sunshine, improved the roads greatly, and while they were at Debub they were able to order in good supplies of grain, which came by truck.

Market towns such as Debub, on the border of Danakil territory, are a wonderful source of information concerning the entire region. People travel in from far and wide, and Nathan was able to note their personal state, and record information about their villages. He interviewed 14 of the 19 district chiefs.

The Barlows learned that there were about 40,000 people in that governmental district. Famine had taken a severe toll. Nathan estimated that about 80 percent of the cattle had died. About two and a half percent of the people had died of starvation. Over 60 percent of the people had been reduced to eating weed seeds, from which they made small, heavy bread cakes.

"How thin and ragged they are!" Doris exclaimed, as the people gathered outside their tent for medical help. It was no wonder. They had had little food, and suffered from many diseases.

Barley harvest was ready at the time. Two men walked to the grain fields with the Barlows and showed them the grain. They pulled off the barley heads and rubbed them in their hands, blowing away the chaff. There were only a few kernels left. What appeared from a distance to be a good crop was only about five percent of normal. At best, it would provide food for maybe two months. Then the people would be faced with hunger again.

As they walked back to their tent, they met a man carrying a goatskin bag over his shoulder.

"This is good," Nathan commented. "He's got grain."

The man stopped and exchanged greetings, and readily showed them the contents of the bag. The Barlows' hopes vanished. The bag contained mostly dirt and chaff. "In a normal harvest," the man said, "we would leave this for the goats."

As they moved about during their survey, they saw the food-for-work program in action. Eleven miles of road were repaired and opened up in two days, under the efforts of about 1000 men. They were all paid in grain.

With the survey completed, the Barlows returned to Makalle, where Nathan finalized his report and made his recommendations. The work they did was to chart the course of the Relief and Rehabilitation workers in that area for many months to come.

11. Dr. Pam

November saw the beginning of a much-needed lull in operations. What harvests there were, provided food for many people for a few weeks at least. The enormous crowds at the shelters were under control and began to thin out as those who were able returned home.

But everyone knew that it was the lull before another storm. So many people were destitute, and had no means to farm in any case, that relief organizations stepped up their preparations for the next wave of disaster. By January or February, the whole cycle would start over again.

During November and December special emphasis was being placed on recruiting relief workers who could stay on the job right through that coming crisis. Funds and supplies from the homelands were coming through well as people responded generously.

SIM opened its fourth relief base, in Makalle, the capital of Tigre province. This was a totally unexpected opportunity. SIM work in northern Ethiopia had been sparse. It was a strong Orthodox and Islamic area, and mission work had not been encouraged there. Most SIM work was in the central and generally southern areas of Ethiopia. George hurried off to consult with Don Stilwell and SIM administration in Addis Ababa.

The Governor did not want SIM to build conventional mission stations. He preferred that the people be reached by mobile clinics. Some villages could be reached by road, others would have to be reached by air, using light aircraft. He asked George where the Mission would like to have airstrips cleared.

To locate the best places, George decided to make an aerial survey. In mid-January, SIM operations received a boost with the arrival of a helicopter. It was provided for a period of about six weeks by the Swiss Helimission, headed by Ernst Tanner, pilot. SIM supplied the fuel, Helimission did the rest. With the helicopter, scores of tasks were performed in a fraction of the time that would have been needed otherwise.

Using the helicopter, George and volunteer medic Dr. Jack Miner of Canada, who at this point was supervising the clinic program, selected sites for 21 airstrips. Many of these were soon leveled and cleared by Ethiopians, under government supervision, in a food-for-work scheme.

To help Dr. Miner as he flitted from clinic to clinic, Dr. Pam arrived from Australia. Her full name was Pamela Williams, but she was always called Dr. Pam. She was a small person, with short dark hair and bright brown eyes. When she got behind the wheel of a Land-Rover, her diminutive form looked strangely out of place. It seemed that some six-foot male should have been steering the vehicle around boulders and over rocks, and changing the tires when they gave out on the mountainous roads.

Her introduction to the Danakils was abrupt — not an uncommon introduction to anything in those days. She arrived at Makalle one day, to learn that she was leaving early next morning by helicopter to investigate a proposed clinic site.

"What an experience, flying down over the escarpment!" she recalled. "The green eucalyptus trees of the highlands just faded away into the dry rocks of the lowland. I wondered why people lived down there. It was a desert."

At the site, Dr. Pam found 70 children in the community, almost all of whom were suffering from the effects of hunger, and anemia from malaria. "The adults seem to be of good stature and fairly well nourished," she observed. "This may be a social rather than a nutritional problem."

The people weren't as friendly as she thought they would be. "What would your reaction be if this helicopter thing dropped out of the sky into your village," the pilot asked "with strange people aboard to look you over and ask you questions?"

Pam agreed that the people had reason to be apprehensive.

Next day she was off again, to a place called Afdera. "There is a great deal of malaria here," she reported. "As a result, the people are anemic and so very thin. And I haven't seen so much TB in my entire life. We should put on some kind of a campaign to get rid of it. The children here should have Fafa to build them up. Lots of it."

The helicopter flew off, leaving Dr. Pam and her team on their own. To her surprise, Dr. Pam learned that they were to stay the night. "I didn't bring anything," she remarked. "I don't even have a sleeping bag!"

Her introduction to relief work was under way! It was all new to Dr. Pam. One of the team men quickly offered her his. She was still apprehensive about spending the night, though. She had heard that the Danakils were fierce people, and she wondered how safe she was, despite the presence of the other team members.

The women and children who had come for medicine quickly disappeared after receiving treatment, but some of the men remained, apparently arguing about what they should do next. Dr. Pam's fears were allayed when she was told that the men were discussing whether they should kill a goat and feed the visitors.

A goat was produced, from somewhere, and killed and cooked right in front of Dr. Pam. Desert hospitality was being observed. After a hot cup of tea, she was shown to a crude shelter where she was to sleep, and provided with a guard to keep away the hyenas, which were already prowling near the camp.

Next morning the helicopter dropped out of the sky to return the team to Makalle. "We had difficulty finding you," the pilot explained. "Low clouds. We dropped a Dutch doctor out here a few weeks ago and couldn't find him for seven days because of low clouds. You're lucky."

As the helicopter flew toward Makalle, one of the team, a government official, spoke with Dr. Pam about his Orthodox religion. "It is meaningless to me," he declared.

"My faith in Jesus Christ means a great deal to me," she replied, and explained how she had accepted Him as her Savior. Her brief encounter was typical of the many ways in which the seed of the gospel was sewn throughout the entire relief operation in northern Ethiopia. It was to produce a remarkable harvest.

Dr. Miner decided that Dr. Pam would be most useful at Debub, which the Barlows had used as one of their survey bases. From there she could also help the medical team at Adi Kai. She was given two Ethiopian nurses, Kebebush and Selas, and the three of them were flown in by helicopter. Gary Eaton, a volunteer whose parents were missionaries in the Philippines, followed with a truckload of food and supplies.

There was a government clinic at Debub, but it had not been staffed for several months. The clinic was one of a circle of buildings that enclosed an enormous village square. On the weekly market day this area was filled with thousands of people who came down out of the surrounding hills. Food shortage was their main topic of discussion.

The medical team unpacked their stuff and opened for business. They soon had their first case. They were led to a hut where a sick boy lay.

"I wonder that he's alive," Pam told her nurses. "He has a bad case of scurvy. Look at his bleeding lips. And he's terribly dehydrated. Ask the father how much water he's had recently."

Dr. Pam had the same problem with language that most volunteers had. She couldn't speak it, or understand it. Everything had to pass through an interpreter. The father told Kebebush, "We haven't had much water to give him. He's had very little for two weeks now."

Dr. Pam used her stethoscope. "He has a chest infection, too," she observed. There were complications in trying to treat him. The father was lame and could not carry water. There was no woman in the house. Dr. Pam decided he would have to be taken to the clinic, where they could give him the local version of "intensive care."

Gary, a husky lad, picked up the wizened patient and carried him to the clinic. The boy had just been made comfortable when he became delirious. The team gave him IV, improvising the equipment when they discovered that all their medical supplies were not in the load.

Gary put up a couple of tents for living quarters, and volunteered to sit with the boy through the night. Candles were lit, the women retired, and Gary kept his vigil, making sure the IV drip stayed in place.

In the morning the boy was able to take fluids by mouth. The team had saved their first patient.

He stayed with them for several days, strengthened with food and vitamins, and Dr. Pam's own oranges. When he was able to live at home, they took him bread and milk. It was two months before he could walk. When he did recover, he spent a great deal of time at the clinic, trying to be helpful.

"Considering the conditions under which we treated him," Dr.

Pam observed, "his recovery was a remarkable success."

There were many remarkable successes at Debub and Adi Kai. Dr. Pam learned a lot about improvisation, substitution, and frustration. "I learned what it is like to do medical work without adequate supplies," she explained. "We also learned to get along without the kind of comfort and food we were used to at home. I learned to enjoy Ethiopian food with my team members, and we got along fine living together."

They treated as many as 120 patients each day. Medical problems were greatly aggravated by the lack of proper food among the people. Grain distribution was a help, but few people really had an adequate diet.

The helicopter service ended just after Dr. Pam's team opened Debub, so supplies had to come by road, and were often delayed. Communication with the main base at Makalle was slow.

At Debub and Adi Kai many people were hearing the gospel for the first time. Each morning as people came for medicine, Kebebush spoke to them from one of Christ's parables, which were admirably appropriate to the Danakils, and made applications to the lives of the hearers.

Some of the more interested people of the village joined the team each evening as they sat in front of the clinic building singing hymns. They were ignorant of Bible truth, and repeatedly asked questions about angels and saints, questions stemming from Islamic and Orthodox backgrounds. It was difficult for them to comprehend how they could go directly to God. One of the most important verses the team used with them was, "Jesus said, I am the way, the truth, and the life. No man cometh to the Father but by me."

Many expressed concern about their spiritual condition, but there was not much open confession of faith.

"Perhaps some of our own employees are hindering the acceptance of the gospel," was the observation made eventually by William Morrow, who was then managing the base at Makalle, and keeping an eye on the medical teams in the districts. He kept Debub and Adi Kai in supplies. "I'm troubled about the fellow who's in charge of grain distribution in this area. The people seem to resent him deeply."

The man in question had actually been beaten once by the people who were receiving grain, and the people were told that if they didn't stop their rough tactics the relief work there would have to be stopped.

On a later visit, William had the answer. "We found that he was charging every person he registered. He was making them pay for free grain. He's been fired."

With that cared for, good relationships were quickly established.

There were always problems with helping people. Corruption appeared everywhere that disaster hit. Men were always ready to step in to make money even if doing so caused extreme suffering and death.

Grain distribution often brought out the worst in people. Some of the most needy were pushed out of line by those who had adequate food in their houses. "People lied blatantly about their needs," Dr. Pam said. "The strongest people shoved their way to the front, taking advantage of the weak ones. Those who had large supplies came begging, or sent their children in rags to say, 'I have no father, no mother.'"

When the relief workers discovered cheating on the part of the people they were trying to help, or dishonesty among some employees, they were very discouraged. "We would feel like giving up," Dr. Pam explained. "But then we saw nurses and other Ethiopians giving themselves without reservation, day and night, and we took heart."

Dr. Pam's days at Debub and Adi Kai were coming to an end. There were larger things looming. Dr. Miner was experiencing physical difficulties with high blood pressure. He had to leave because of the high altitudes. This was a blow. The Miners had never been in a work that brought them so much satisfaction.

The Relief and Rehabilitation board named Dr. Pam as his replacement. She was soon on the road in her Land-Rover, supervising clinics in many parts of Tigre province. Her time at Debub had prepared her well.

12. The desert

The early months of 1974 saw the relief program shift into high gear and stay there. More and more people and organizations around the world were lending their aid. Churches and concerned individuals gave generously through SIM.

When the meager harvests were eaten up, the famine conditions returned. But this time relief programs were better organized. They didn't have all their problems solved, by any means, but they avoided the enormous anguish of the previous summer.

Everyone was working flat out, as the Australian volunteers put it, to keep ahead of the feeding and medical programs. Wollo province again suffered more than Tigre. But in Tigre, the medical side of the work was growing rapidly. The mobile clinics were increasing in number among the Danakils, and SIM was learning a great deal about the Danakils that would be of great help in the days ahead.

Little missionary work had been done among these people, and SIM had only marginal contact. The Red Sea Mission Team worked among them, and Christian Missions in Many Lands also reached them in a small way. The famine opened an entirely new territory to SIM ministry, both geographically and culturally. The Danakils were a distinctively different people.

One of the relief workers who observed the Danakils firsthand was Marilyn Mehalich. She arrived in Ethiopia in March as part of a 16-volunteer team from Seattle Pacific College in USA. That team stayed for two months, sponsored by Medical Assistance Programs. It was one of many teams that helped out under the auspices of many fine organizations.

Marilyn was in nurse's training, but did not yet have her degree. She was assigned as a medical worker to a team of four, to an outpost at a place with the intriguing name of DigDig Sahala. The team was flown in, with the assurance that the plane would supply them each week.

They set up a clinic in the middle of the desert, with volcanic craters all around them. "We chose a site that had the most acacia trees," Marilyn reported with a grin. "We pitched the clinic tent under one of them, and another tent under the other. At that point we ran out of trees."

They soon were busy with medical work and making surveys of food and water conditions. The Danakils, they noted, were a very slender people. The men wore long, wraparound skirts or loincloths, with a large knife prominent at the waist. The daggers were not curved, but the blade made an obtuse angle, the apex of which was the center of gravity of the weapon.

To the Danakils, the camel is the most useful and beautiful creature God created. And they believe in God and creation. They are almost all Muslims. Their tempers flare easily, and feuds are settled with their ever-present knives. The great tragedy of the famine, to them, was that their camels were dying.

"The temperature was about 115 degrees every day," Marilyn wrote. "The water supply was very poor, but the people took care of us. They placed guards outside our tents to chase away the hyenas at night. They were receptive to the medicine we provided. The nearest people to us lived about a mile away in a half a dozen huts, but people came to us from far away by camel, donkey, mule, and on foot."

Marilyn learned a lot about medical problems. "I've seen things I'll never see in ordinary nursing, and experienced things I'll probably never experience again, unless I return," she said.

But medical work was not Marilyn's only concern. "I've grown much in the Lord because of the experiences in the desert. The people were eager to hear the gospel, which we shared with them each evening."

There were days when they were without water and ran out of canned food. They ate camel meat and goat meat and drank camel's milk. They observed that the Danakils lived on this kind of food without suffering. In fact, Marilyn noted, they seemed enormously strong... until they got sick.

Of all the complications of living in the desert, the greatest was the matter of water.

"The Danakils seem to get along with very little water," Marilyn reported. "They do not waste water bathing, or washing utensils or clothing. They rub butter on their clothing and their bodies, and this eliminates the need for bathing. The butter lubricates their bodies and slows the rate of evaporation of body fluids. It also partially protects them from vermin."

Although they tried to keep certain waterholes in the sand for their animals, the people shared most water supplies with their cattle. Camels, goats, and donkeys waded into the muddy water and polluted it. The people filled their water bags with the water, which contained parasites, worms, and bacteria. They drank it without boiling it.

Although the Danakils did not drink much water, the relief workers needed it. The desert was as foreign to the Ethiopians as it was to Marilyn.

"We boiled all our drinking water for at least 20 minutes " Marilyn said. "We had to drink large quantities to keep up with the evaporation from our bodies. We had to depend on the people for our water supply, and they couldn't understand why we needed so much.

"Sometimes they left us burning with thirst. We tried to borrow their water skins and their animals so we could draw our own, but they wouldn't let us use their animals. I don't know what we would have done, though, if they had agreed to let us use a camel. Where does one start?"

Marilyn was glad that none of her party got sick. She was concerned about the drinking water, despite the precautions they took. It tasted terrible. They were glad for the brine and syrup in the canned foods they had. "We drank it, not because it tasted good, but because it was liquid."

Sometimes the feeling of being beyond hope was strong. They looked at the endless, treeless desert around them, barren of anything that might suggest water, and found it frightening. They thought of the Danakils, for whom this was normal. What did they do when the few waterholes dried up? There seemed such a small margin between life and death.

Marilyn noted that the Danakils, accustomed to the harshness of desert life, did not suffer from the drought as severely as did the people of the highlands. "On the other hand," she noted, "they could be pretty callous about neighbors who were starving. It may be that they thought that persons who couldn't survive the famine should be allowed to die... a very fatalistic attitude. Or perhaps they just took care of themselves first. It was hard to tell."

The plane came every week but one. That day the little camp was "fogged in" by dust and the pilot couldn't find it. On some trips, the team was flown to other locations for medical work.

The team saw the religious side of the Danakils. "They seem to be strong Muslims," Marilyn wrote. "They practice their religion. They go down to the dry riverbed where there are traces of grass, and they pray there in a group every morning at sunrise, and again about three in the afternoon, and at six in the evening. They chant parts of the Koran, though they seemingly don't understand it, since it is in Arabic.

"They were very devout when they observed Muhammed's birthday. They prayed and fasted for three days and nights. Then they had a celebration for a day and a night. They sang and beat their drums continuously."

Marilyn thought of a different aspect to their religion when she recalled that strict Muslims do not drink alcoholic beverages. "Some of these drank alcohol," she noted. "And they chewed chat, which I think you would call a drug. It is a weed. The highlanders grow it and sell it to the Danakils. They get together for chat chewing sessions and chew themselves into a kind of stupor. It is a depressant."

The team was concerned about crops and the prospect of getting a harvest. But the Danakils seemed to live off their animals. The team saw no cultivation at all. The people used a lot of grain in their bread, but they got it by trading chunks of salt from desert deposits, and of course, their animals.

The division of labor favored the men. The women spend a lot of time kneeling on the dirt floor of their huts, made of skin-covered poles, grinding grain on flat stones. The evening meal was the main one. The boys and girls took care of the herds, and sometimes the men drove them to water. But generally the men gathered in groups in the shade to discuss their affairs, which included raiding other territory.

"They seemed lazy and proud," the team reported, "except when they got into fights. They are very emotional, and quickly excited."

When their time was up, and the team was flown back to Makalle, they had done a nice piece of pioneering. They had careful observations of conditions in the area, they had helped many people medically, and they had introduced the gospel.

Just before she left Ethiopia to return home, Marilyn said, "I would like to see SIM and other missions open regular missionary work among the Danakils. They seemed so open, and they need the gospel."

13. Diary

The workers who arrived early in 1974 found a rapidly growing network of relief centers. The emphasis was on meeting the needs of people where they were, and no new shelters were being erected along the great road. The existing shelters were more or less equal to the wave of refugees, which had peaked during the late summer.

By this time, the work was known simply as R&R — Relief and Rehabilitation. Relief work, meeting immediate needs, was merging into Rehabilitation — getting things back to normal and trying to keep them there.

R&R volunteers were made up of a great cross section of people, from many countries. A lot of them were young people, students or recent graduates, quite a few of them from Bible schools or colleges. Some were optimistic about everything that happened in R&R work, others were analytical, some were more emotional than others, many were ready for theological discussion any time of the day or night.

Noel Magor arrived in Addis Ababa from Australia on December 22, 1973. He spent Christmas there with SIM missionaries, and then was sent to Alamatta. His immediate task was the purchasing of grain. Grain was needed in great quantities. It was in Alamatta and distributed from there. He would buy it in the local markets, where there was plenty for sale. He would also start digging wells, to improve local drinking water supplies.

Noel had just completed a course in Agricultural Science at Adelaide University. He was not a farm boy, but he loved everything that had to do with raising plants and animals.

He also had a great concern for people. So much so, that even while he was studying agricultural science, he was thinking of working with young people in coffee houses, and aiding in the rehabilitation of drug addicts. At university he went along with the life style of the moderate element. His hair was not down to his shoulders, but it was long enough to make him look like a character from Dickens. A friend had asked him if he would be interested in helping with famine relief in Ethiopia — and could he have a reply by nine the next morning?

Noel was taken completely by surprise. He went to the Lord in prayer, and spent time reading his Bible that night. Among other passages that he read was Matthew 25:35,"For I was an hungred, and ye gave me meat..."

Next morning he said yes, and in short order was at Alamatta. He kept a diary, in which he recorded his feelings as well as his activities. These excerpts reflect the experiences, problems, and joys of many workers who, like Noel, plunged into relief work in a strange country.

January 21, 1974. I was really looking forward to receiving some mail. None came. It was quite a disappointment.

About 6 p.m. a helicopter arrived carrying George Middleton and Ken Radach. It landed right on the station. Everyone from Alamatta town streamed onto the compound, over fences, through the gate to see this particular breed of aircraft.

It was 11:30 before I got to see George. I wanted to begin grain buying from the villages that still had some to sell, and I wanted his permission to start digging wells. Permission was granted. Praise God for the way He uplifts and protects His own.

January 22. When I went to buy grain I felt completely ignorant. First we went to several merchants and asked them how much they wanted for teff. They would not tell us. So I stood behind one of them as he weighed and bought grain from the local farmers. I learned that he was making a neat profit on us. It is hard to accept this anomaly that in the midst of crowds of starving people there is plenty of grain, but the hungry people have no money with which to buy it.

A good day, but tired out. One thing, out here the clothes I wear would seem ridiculous back home, but I enjoy wearing them.

In the morning Ato Asafa of the Save the Children Fund, which also has work in Alamatta, asked me for some of the cards we use in our relief program. That was great, as we can coordinate their distribution with our Fafa distribution.

January 23. Today Yemanee, my helper, and I went to Jahan to buy grain. We set up the scales. I was not yet used to buying grain, which today came slowly. Once the people realized that we were offering a fair price, they came. God seems to be giving me jobs which lead me to deal with people. I really enjoy it.

January 25. We are needing 330 tons of teff plus sorghum for our feeding program. At the present rate of one quintal (220 pounds) a day we will never get it. In the villages it is too slow. We must deal in the weekly town market.

January 26. Market day. What is going to happen? Yemanee and myself went down prepared to pay $13 for a quintal of teff and $10.50 per quintal for sorghum. Things started slowly at first but gradually the people crowded around. I weighed, recorded, and looked up the price. Yemanee wrote down the figures and paid the money. It was flat out.

Spent $1500 for the grain we bought. I had an experience with Ato Muhammed and the villagers about our being Christians in the true sense. They said we are always honest. In the evening Eric Svenssen, Ernie Harbidge and I hit the town and bought some Cokes.

We need to pray about the grain buying, as 330 tons is a lot. The whole grain setup bothers us. Rich merchants have bought grain from farmers in areas where there is no famine and have brought it here to sell at prices starving people cannot afford. It seems they could make some effort to keep the prices lower.

January 27. Sunday. Was one of those really needed days... a day of rest.

January 31. Leaving the diary for a few days makes events hard to recall. This week has been so hectic and tiring that I haven't had time to write. I think I'll address today's activities to God.

Lord, you know I went to Quoram today to buy grain, and you blessed the whole situation with 33 tons of peas at $15.50 per quintal. After the tremendous excitement of that (especially considering that $15 was the market price), I mentioned it to one of our men and got the unenthusiastic response that the merchants will be making $150 on the deal. Well, I couldn't get him lower.

Lord, I came out here because you called me, and then I get so run off my feet that I don't even have the time to have devotions for the day. I'm losing my compassion for the people. I'm physically exhausted and, Lord, even thinking spiritual is an effort. People are becoming objects Lord, I feel lonely. Lord, I beg you that you will rekindle my love for you and for people.

Thanks for answers to prayer: Yesterday chloramphenicol tablets arrived. We had waited for weeks for them. And also, Lord, for the grain buying. You softened Ato Muhammed's heart to sell at a price you gave me wisdom to ask. Father, I love you in such an immature way, and my love for my fellow-men often fails.

February 1. We went to Quoram to continue the purchasing of peas. Ernie drove the truck and I the Toyota. When we arrived we found Beyena and ran into a few problems. We had brought our own workers to put the grain in bags. Beyena had his workers, who wanted to do the same job. They refused to leave. What was I to do? I told Beyena that if he wanted his men to do the job, he would have to pay them. A big uproar followed. Still the men wouldn't leave.

Since I was the "union official" I dreaded a strike policy, a bluff. "Ato Beyena, unless your men get out of the storeroom immediately, I will pack up the scales and leave with no grain." Finally the men left, reluctantly.

February 2. Market day in Alamatta! We arrived in the market about 7:30 a.m. and set up our starting price at $12.25. Most of the people who brought grain to sell rejected our price. We raised to $12.50 and the grain started to come in. Our pile grew faster than those of the merchants. The Lord certainly blessed us.

February 3. The morning was a real wrestle to get to my knees, but when I did and when I confessed my lack of devotion to Himself, and when I thanked Him for His faithfulness, the alienation was removed and peace restored. Later in the morning I was approached about taking some evangelists to Rahay. I didn't want to, but in the end I did. As Ken Radach said in the evening, a person must not just commit his future to the Lord but that very moment in which the struggle is going on.

During the early part of the afternoon, Heather Bobbermein, a nurse from the clinic, and I shared all our gripes and then prayed about them. It is important that Christians bear one another's burdens, especially when each is experiencing the same problem. A letter came from dad. Some of what he wrote was so strengthening. Praise the Lord!

February 5. In the evening I spent an hour doing dishes. I want the Lord to teach me a true meekness. The Lord needs to teach me not to grumble about the jobs I've got to do and the food I'm given, which at times isn't the best. Thanks, Lord, for another day.

February 6. I used the tractor this morning. A bit of a stir. Where do you put the water? Oh, Noel, you don't drive with the trailer brake on! I'm learning.

Tadessa and I worked together driving the tractor and collecting charcoal. I learned how to carry bags of charcoal on my back. We use it to cook food and to boil our drinking water. Propane gas is often unavailable.

February 7. Today the beggars seemed to be more demanding than usual at Mai Chau where we had gone to buy grain. I find that one of the most difficult things to take out here is begging. It seems so degrading to human beings. Yet I guess that in some cases it is justified, where there are disabled people with no support.

Back at Alamatta, I found that Ernie had done a deal with a merchant for the purchase of 1000 quintals of grain at $12.25. Praise the Lord! This was a real answer to prayer. Towards evening I decided to try the discs. Tizzy had to show me how to disengage the trailer with the hydraulics. I set the discs at an acute angle to increase depth and then proceeded to try them. Then someone noticed a crack in a disc. I felt a fool.

But then we found that the disc had already had a three-inch crack in it. It wasn't due to my driving after all.

When I was plowing, I said to Pete, "Do I look like a farmer?" "No," said Pete, "you look like a long-haired university student."

February 8. George Middleton came in the morning and it was good to see him. We got on well together. We talked about projects in reforestation, plowing, village rehabilitation, and village gardens. He was quite encouraging.

February 10 Sunday. I drove Ken Radach to Dessie. On the way we had a good talk about many things. He is keen on work with Muslim people. He is concerned about keeping up our evangelistic work while engaging in famine relief.

On the way back to Alamatta, Bill, a guy with the Peace Corps, came with me. He asked me about the aims of SIM and about God, and I was able to share my faith with him.

February 12. Work began early today and finished late. Yemanee came around to get $1000 for the merchant for grain. So I took it into town. Time was made after this for prayer. At times, with the pressure of getting jobs done, little things tend to be annoying and by getting down on one's knees for a while, burdens can be lifted.

A cup of coffee followed before I took the truck down to the airstrip with pipes for dragging the surface. But the pipes rolled. We tried a harrow and it worked better. I was ready for tea, when I found the men uptight. They had no food all day. Some was sent out, but they did not get any. A hundred bags of grain were still sitting in the market. So Mick and I drove out, fed the workers and gave them blankets. Most of the men stayed to guard the grain.

At times during the day I was really frustrated. Lord, teach me patience. Help me to control my tongue and to speak in love always.

February 21. An item for which to praise the Lord — the head merchant with whom we have been dealing wants to become a follower of Jesus. He was a Muslim because his father and grandfather were Muslims. He saw that we had something that he wanted. Today he wanted to read the Bible and learn about our faith. Yemaneee has been witnessing to him. What an encouragement, that the work required in being a merchant and buying grain could lead to his conversion.

February 22 (SIM monthly day of prayer). I had to arrange signatures for permission to dig a well on private property. I met the farmer, who was quite disagreeable. He wanted to get paid for the water that came from the well. We wanted a written agreement that the water was to be free. We went to the drilling site but he was "no go." When I suggested going to court, he decided to give us the land. So we signed the agreement with three witnesses.

Before hopping into the car to go back, I picked up a Gospel and prayed for an opportunity to witness to the government secretary who had come with us on the well business. When he got into the car he picked up the Gospel and began to read it. I was able to talk to him about Christ. He wants a teacher in his village so that he can learn more about the Bible.

The man from whom we acquired the well-drilling site used to be very rich. He had ten oxen before the famine and much land. When the famine came all his oxen and other cattle died. Now to support his family, a wife, and five children he makes charcoal and sells it. He is now a poor man.

I was really tired in the evening but the prayer meeting refreshed me. I was going to miss it due to tiredness, but woke and had a great time with the Lord.

February 23. In the evening before supper I spent some time with Ernie and Rod Loewen, Alamatta station manager, discussing hair. As a result I decided to have mine cut. I don't want to be a spectacle all the while I am here. Had a good stir with Willene, Rod's wife, as she hacked it off while Rod made wise comments.

Rod and I talked about Scripture memorization. I must get into this as the Lord is giving me a hunger for His Word. I started by learning Psalm 1.

February 24 (Sunday). Today Yemanee and I went to Waja for a service, taking with us some girls to sing. On previous occasions Daniel and Woldi had been forbidden to preach, under the threat of being put into jail. Despite this threat, we went to the market and Getachu spoke first.

"Do you remember me?" he asked.

"Yes," the people replied.

"Who have we brought the grain for?" he asked.

"For us," the villagers replied.

Then he told them how we loved them, and from there he preached the gospel. About 200 people were listening, and there was evidence of conviction and agreement with all that was said. They want us to come every week to teach them.

When we were finished with the service, we began to hand out Gospels and tracts. There was such a rush and grabbing for the tracts that we had to stop. We tried again but we were pushed against the car. We got into the car and gave away a few more tracts before leaving the people whose hands were still outstretched.

March 1. The old woman whose land we plowed used to be rich until her husband died. Relatives sold all her oxen so that she has no way to plow her fields. She showed us the grass seed she was eating.

Tadessa was preaching in Rahay today to several hundred people who were being registered to receive grain. Some Orthodox priests disturbed the meeting. Then the people said, "We want to hear Tadessa's teaching, because when we were in need, he helped us." Thank you, Lord, for the way we've been able to express our love to the people.

March 5. When I was out for plowing supervision in the afternoon, a rich man invited me into his home. He offered me curdled milk. I refused the milk and told him that I couldn't stomach it. He insisted, so I began to drink my full cup of milk with lumps. It was sour. I tried to swallow as much as possible without swilling it around in my mouth. The milk had a strong flavor of smoke. I got through the whole glass slowly. What a triumph! Everybody on our compound is awaiting my diarrhea.

March 7. I was up at 5:20 to get ready for plowing with the tractor. I began to think of something else. Our monster was beating the ox to his job. The ox needed to eat and drink before going to the field. Our machine was being satisfied with a heady supply of diesel fuel and was being lubricated by its circulating black blood.

Yet an ox is living and has character compared to our insensitive hunk of steel. But I should not be too harsh in condemning it as the product of Western technology. It was a source of hope to these desperate people. A machine which we of the West curse for its noise and pollution was bringing life to a ravaged land.

March 26. Today is tractor repair day. Problem: the steering was too tight. There was an adjustment screw but it was in an inaccessible place. Oh, well. It looks like everything will have to be taken to bits again.

One of the problems in this area is the lack of motivation among the people for survival and self-improvement. The men are very lazy. Family ties are not strong enough to motivate a husband to work hard to provide for his family. The husband deserts and leaves wife and children destitute and dependent on relief.

The men sit back and wait for the tractor to plow their fields, when they could pick up their hoes and try to do a little work by hand. The rich farmers are finding it it difficult to hire men to help in the fields. The villagers are saying, Why should we work when we can receive free grain? Just at the moment in the village of Tau I can count ten men. Why aren't they working and providing for their families?

There is sufficient grain in this country and yet people are starving. Tons of grain for distribution were bought in Alamatta, but people will soon be starving there. Starvation is not altogether due to a lack of rain. It is also associated with social conditions among the people.

Family structure is important in society as is community concern. It is well known that in one village well-off people can live next door to starving neighbors. If an aid worker arrived in the village and by chance went to the rich man's home, the rich man would make no mention of his starving neighbor.

The gospel is needed in this country.

14. Fafa camp

Combating malnutrition, particularly in children, was a slow task. It could not be hurried. Their bodies needed time to benefit from nourishment. In the shelters, adults could be given whole grain or flour, which they could grind or cook once they were strong enough to help themselves.

But the little ones needed more than that. Fafa was the answer. It was nourishing, and those who received it quickly showed improvement. Fafa was also the answer for adults, particularly the aged, who had suffered severe malnutrition.

Fafa camps were set up near the shelters. Clinic workers examined the patients and prescribed Fafa if needed. Those who were to receive Fafa were registered and given a pink slip as a ration card. It was handed in each day, marked, and returned. When 20 days were up, the Fafa treatment ended. It could be renewed at the discretion of the clinic workers.

My husband, Mal, sent me to visit the Fafa camp at Alamatta early in 1974. As we came to the area, fenced off with barbed wire, we saw the gray crowds of people inside. They were clothed in rags and tatters. It seemed unfortunate to use barbed wire to keep people in their place, but seeing the crowd milling and pushing about, it became evident that this was about the only way to keep a semblance of order.

We waited a few minutes until the guard opened the gate. We accompanied Kasai, a Christian man if ever there was one, as he wheeled a barrow full of cream-colored Fafa into the enclosure.

There was a great clamor. The wheelbarrow and we were surrounded. It seemed almost impossible to move.

We were in the first section of the enclosure. Over there was the second section, empty, where the people would receive the food. A few school-children pushed the crowd back to make room for the wheelbarrow to move. The ground was rough. It was not easy to get it through the chattering, pushing throng.

As we moved along, women with outstretched hands pleaded with me in Amharic, showing me dirty, thin babies on their backs. Several old men were very insistent, plucking my arm, peering into my face. "Mama!" they called. "Mama!"

Kasai, calm and unruffled as he walked backwards, barrow handles in his strong hands, came to my rescue. "She is a stranger," he told them. "She cannot feed you." He smiled encouragement to the people, showing great patience with them, even though they gave him so little space. He didn't spill any of the precious food, though the barrow was nearly full.

We made it to the empty enclosure, entered, and shut the gate behind us. Kasai set the barrow down and began drawing lines on the ground with a stick. In the first enclosure, the registrar was lining the people up and checking their pink slips against his book.

I wondered what the lines were for. One was drawn the full width of the enclosure. About five feet behind it another was drawn, until the whole area was marked off.

Then the gate was opened and the first woman came in, with her three children. She carried a dirty woven grass basket and an empty fruit juice can. She sat on the line on the ground, nearest to the barrow. Her children crowded behind her. Then came the next woman, and the next, and the next.

Suddenly the attendants at the gate were pushed aside and the mob rushed through. Miraculously they skirted the barrow and took their places along the lines.

Young and old, mothers with children, and fathers with children were there. Old men huddled together in family groups. They were all dirty, gray, tattered, and ragged. No new clothes, or clean clothes were to be seen. Not a pair of shoes was in sight.

The children were skinny, although some at the breast were fairly chubby. The older ones watched with shining eyes as the ladle went back and forth from can to barrow to can. Apparently the ration was one ladlefull per child.

The first woman's can was filled. The children's fingers were in it immediately, dipping out the porridge-like mixture and carrying it to their mouths. The cream-colored mix was about like oatmeal. It was a high protein food and those who ate it regularly gained strength and vitality. They didn't put on a lot of weight, but they developed strong bodies. The people realised this, so the crowd of three or four hundred kept coming back day after day.

"Are there more here today than a week ago?" I asked.

"I don't think so. The numbers seem to be decreasing."

"Is it like last summer?" I asked.

"Oh, no, not like last summer," was the answer. And one could see that in his heart was the same question that was in all our hearts — will the rains be sufficient this year to give good crops and end this time of hunger?

I followed the barrow as it moved along the lines. The food level was going down as Kasai slowly but methodically filled the cans. All sizes and shapes of cans were there, from the kitchens of the missionaries and from the merchants in town.The cans were preferred to gourds. They were easier to keep clean.

I asked Kasai, "Is there no time given to explain that this food is given in the name of Jesus? Do they not give thanks for the food?"

He looked puzzled, as if to say, "How can one do that in the midst of this crowd, plucking and calling and hungry?"

I felt, too, that it was probably impossible, but I had an idea. Among the crowd were some of the older orphans from their camp. They were showing people where to sit, and generally trying to be helpful. One spoke English.

"Can you help me sing the song we sang under the tree this morning?" I asked him. "The one that went, 'Thank you, Jesus'?"

So we got started, about three of us, but before we had reached the fourth short verse, eight or ten of us were singing it. It was in Amharic, a very simple song. As we sang, some turned to us and smiled. A few more caught the idea as we moved along, and we sang, "Thank you, thank you, Jesus... for loving us... for dying for us... for the bread of life..."

Some of the verses were unknown to me, but at least I could sing along, and together we were heard above the chatter of the people. They listened to us, but the wheelbarrow continued to be the center of attention.

Another cook's helper came through the gate and added a huge pail of porridge to the barrow. As the people were fed, the cards and pink slips were given back to them.

I had been so surrounded by the people, with some insistent old women breathing in my face, that suddenly I felt stifled. I wanted out. I felt as though I were breathing sickness. I tried to make my way toward the gate. A group of women prevented me.

They stretched out their bony hands, putting them right in front of my face. One older woman showed me the thinness of her arms, another gestured to tell me she was nearly blind. Eventually a well-dressed Ethiopian teacher came to my rescue. We inched toward the gate, walking backward, which seemed to be the only way to make progress.

Outside the gate the registrar showed me a handful of pink slips. "These won't be given back," he explained. "These people have finished their time. They can come once more tomorrow and I will give them their final allotment of grain. Then we will send them home."

By this time, a second distribution was taking place. Another wheelbarrow had arrived, this one loaded with injera. The children retreated as the adults held out their hands. Those with shawls held them out over two extended arms, so the injera could be placed on them. One injera per adult was the ration, plus half for each child. Each injera was about the size of a large pizza, folded in quarters like a thick, soft cloth.

As it was given out, here and there a smile broke out, and a head nodded in thanks. Once the injera was given out, the people stood up and tied their rags about them. They made their way out the gate and down the paths toward their villages.

"At the end of the alloted time," the registrar explained, "we give them about 12 pounds of grain per adult, and about four and a half per child, and send them home, telling them they should now try and take care of themselves. But it doesn't always work right. In about three days they often come back saying they are hungry.

"It's difficult to know if they really need food or if they just want free food. They might sell the injera or the grain. Sometimes they don't know how to cook the grain properly. Look at that boy, for an example."

We looked at a boy who seemed to be about 12 years old.

"He doesn't know how to cook grain. He's getting better, but his parents have died. He can't cook for himself. He needs to be given food until he can somehow get back on a farm with some relatives. But he doesn't know where they are. It is a hard problem.''

Famine relief is made up of many problems, we concluded. Every person receiving Fafa or injera that day was a problem. How can they be shaken loose from dependence on relief measures? How can they learn to take care of themselves once again?

Relief is fine, but rehabilitation has to be the final answer.

15. Shifting gears

Don Stilwell and the members of the R&R board in Addis Ababa had been looking ahead. They had been thinking hard about the coming summer. No one knew if rain would come, but if it did, there was a lot of work to be done. Thousands of people were unable to farm.

The rain would not produce crops that had not been sown. Without those crops, thousands of people would continue in their state of dependence on handouts of food.

But how could they farm without oxen? How could they plow? How could they sow without seed grain? Most of them had eaten it. And what about health problems? They would recur with fierce intensity if drinking water were polluted. And how could people be sent back to their villages, weak and susceptible to disease, when preventive health measures were virtually unknown?

The answers were not easy. But one thing was crystal clear. Phase Two of the R&R program would have to be pushed hard, and quickly. People were still hungry, and they were being fed, but unless they were rehabilitated in the next few months, at least to the extent of being able to farm, they would face another year without a harvest. Famine relief would have to move in again.

The board decided to shift gears. From here in, emphasis would have to be on rehabilitation, rather than relief. Reliable information was on hand concerning the situation in many areas. There were reports on the number of plowing oxen that had died, and how many were still available. There were reports on how many people there were in the villages, and how many had able-bodied males.

R&R would now have four major thrusts: medical work, agriculture, food and grain distribution, and water supply.

Medical work was well under way, with the many clinics already functioning, but in light of the enormity of public health problems, many more were needed.

Agriculture needed a great deal of assistance. There were many ways in which the people could be helped produce more and better crops. New crops could be introduced. Improved seeds could be used. Simple tools could be distributed. New tools could be introduced, fertilizers could be used. Fields could be plowed by tractor.

Grain distribution was essential, because it meant the difference between life and death for thousands. It would be increasingly tied into the other projects, though, as payment for work. A lot of work related to water supply, for example, could be paid for in grain. Digging wells and making simple irrigation channels needed a lot of labor.

The water project received a tremendous boost in mid-February with the arrival from England of a mobile well-drilling rig. This huge piece of equipment, mounted on a truck, was donated by The Evangelical Alliance Relief (TEAR) Fund, and the Christoffel Blindenmission. It was purchased at a cost of $100,000.

Transporting the rig from England to Ethiopia was a problem. The Suez Canal was closed, and sending it around the Cape would take months. The answer came in the form of the Royal Air Force, which flew it out for a reasonable fee. It was not an easy job to load the massive truck and drilling rig into the transport plane, but it was done, and the plane delivered it to Addis Ababa.

It was assembled and made operational, then driven north, by three RAF officers who volunteered their vacation time for the job.

In mid-March, after the usual unavoidable delays in getting customs clearance for the machine, making the necessary adjustments and assemblies, and tests, they drilled their first well, at Fingal Guma, near Alamatta. It was a great day, and the beginning of a new chapter in the development of many towns and villages.

As more volunteers became available, teams were organized with various goals in view. Some would plow fields for people who had no means of their own. Some would distribute seed grain to those who had none. Some would dig wells and show local people how to do likewise.

All this put R&R in need of more equipment. The teams needed vehicles to move around in, tents to live in, foodstuffs, medical supplies, fuel for their vehicles, radios for communication, plows, tractors for plowing, trailers to haul goods, equipment for drilling and digging wells.

People with new skills were also needed — agriculturists, hydrologists, people with experience in many fields. It would also require more hands and feet, people to get to work on the village level, do manual labor, drive vehicles, maintain them, and build whatever needed building.

A priority need was for a corps of key people to organize programs, coordinate them, and generally administer the work in its several districts.

SIM transferred as many people as it could spare to R&R, but they were not enough. Don Stilwell sent requests to the homelands for managers. "They can be short termers," he said, "but we need them right now."

Terry Norr and Carlyle Dewey were the first to respond to the plea for administrative help. Terry was working in conservation in British Columbia, Canada, when he heard of the need. He and his wife, Jan, decided to get involved.

Carlyle was from Minneapolis, USA. Administration was his field. His Ph.D. qualified him for college administration or teaching political science. He and his wife had a deep interest in missions. They looked upon the appeal from Ethiopia as a call from God.

Terry and Carlyle arrived in Addis Ababa within a few days of each other, and were soon carrying responsibilities in the R&R work. When projects such as digging wells, placing windmills on them, planting seed, or building roads or airstrips were approved, Terry arranged for the purchase and delivery of materials to the sites.

R&R workers sent out from the homelands were teamed up with Ethiopian counterparts who were being recruited from churches in Ethiopia. Most of them came from SIM-related churches in Asmara, Addis Ababa, and the south. Many of the Ethiopians were teachers, high school or university students, paramedics, or could keep accounts, work on inventories, or drive and service vehicles.

Most of them had a zeal to witness. They added their own testimonies and instruction to that of the foreigners with whom they worked. Because of their language advantage, they often did far more personal and public witnessing than their partners from overseas.

The team members readily shared their experiences and taught each other their skills. That was one beauty of the partner scheme. Scores of Ethiopians learned things that enabled them to keep the program moving when the overseas volunteers went home again. Warm friendships developed between foreign volunteers and Ethiopian ones.

The united witness of the R&R workers began to have its impact. It was obvious that there were responsive hearts among the many sufferers who had been helped. "Rice Christians" there would be — those who professed conversion in hopes of getting better treatment or some other advantage — but it was not difficult to discern most of them. What really stirred the R&R workers was the wholesome response by people who had not known the gospel, but who saw the message of love lived out in the actions of the workers, and who, hearing and understanding their message, committed themselves to Jesus Christ.

This was unheard of in northern Ethiopia. Converts had been few, indeed, in this Islamic and Orthodox area. It was not an easy thing to make a break from traditional ways. It was not easy, famine or not, to go against the pattern of culture and community life.

But one by one, and two by two, here and there throughout the many R&R locations, Ethiopians confessed Jesus Christ as Savior. Around Alamatta, there were a number of conversions among people who were not adversely affected by famine. They were town people, whose lives were not disrupted by poverty or hunger. Some of them were working at the R&R centers, employed by SIM or government.

In mid-March, 20 of them were baptized at Alamatta — a major spiritual breakthrough. At Fingal Guma, where the first deep well had been drilled by the TEAR rig, 40 conversions were reported in April.

The spiritual potential of the program, in addition to the essential human needs it was meeting, inspired a major plan in George Middleton's mind. He talked it over with the R&R board, and headed home to Canada.

His hope was to recruit up to 100 students from Bible schools and colleges and similar institutions, and get them out to Ethiopia as soon as they left school in June. Each student would be a sound Christian, capable of contributing to the spiritual ministry. Each one would sign up for a full year. Each one would be financially supported by a church, or friends, or whoever. Each one would be assigned an Ethiopian partner.

George's plan would solve a number of major problems. Short term workers had done a fantastic job. They had saved the day, no doubt about it. But the shorter the term, the more travel expense was involved. There was more scheduling needed, more internal travel and supervision required.

People on one-year assignments would not place as huge a load on administration and service and supply. They would also have more time to minister spiritually. They would be more effective with their Ethiopian partners, by spending enough time with them.

The Christian media in USA and Canada were getting out the news that skilled technicians, nurses, doctors, and people to do general work were urgently needed.

When George made a whirlwind tour through western Canada and parts of the USA, he hoped to find two or three or four from each school. Instead, they came forward in tens and twenties. The schools backed them up enthusiastically. They formed school teams, and the student bodies got behind them financially. Churches and youth groups and businessmen and many others rallied to provide the funds they needed.

As a result, over 70 volunteers were recruited to go to Ethiopia! George flew back to Ethiopia to make plans to receive them.

The volunteers would come in to the country at Asmara, where George was based. He rented a hotel large enough to accommodate the whole group. Orientation would be brief but concentrated, and the whole group taught at once. Don Stilwell, Terry Norr, and Carlyle Dewey burned the midnight oil planning assignments and the flow of supplies.

That was when the Ghinda tragedy struck. Guerrillas of the Eritrean Liberation Front attacked the hospital of the Orthodox Presbyterian Church at Ghinda, in the far north. They shot and killed one missionary nurse, Anna Strikwerder, and kidnapped another, Debbie Dortzbach. News of the tragedy appeared on TV and radio and in newspapers all over the world. The political situation in the north became tense. The ELF was also holding some American oil company employees as hostages.

Asmara is the capital of Eritrea. Further moves by the ELF might jeopardize R&R work and workers in the area. SIM officers in USA and Canada were urged by government representatives not to send R&R workers to Asmara. In Ethiopia, USA and Canadian embassies warned their people not to travel outside Asmara. SIM agreed not to take a chance.

The reception and orientation program was switched to the capital, Addis Ababa. R&R staff there had two days in which to get ready for the first group, which numbered 35. They had to find sleeping quarters, arrange for meals, and for briefing sessions.

A house was rented, and hurriedly equipped for sleeping, cooking, and eating. The day the group arrived they were welcomed by the Canadian ambassador, as well as SIM staff, and quickly settled in. The house became the unplanned R&R base in Addis Ababa.

In short order the volunteers were on their way to their assignments. A new chapter had begun.

16. Water

In May and June several significant things happened. Widespread early rains had been reported earlier in many of the drought-stricken areas, and help had been given to get seed into the ground.

Some places did not receive rain. The people in those places continued in their famine condition.

In Wollo, SIM had two tractors running constantly, plowing fields for widows and other destitute people. Several important water projects were under way. Feeder roads on a food-for-work basis were opening new areas. Airstrips were increasing in number.

And much farther north, in Eritrea province, a new area had been opened — Af Abet. This barren, rocky, hot, dry place had seen an SIM station opened in 1962. The work had been small, and very, very slow. The people were Muslims, and expressed little interest in the gospel message.

The drought had made life even more difficult than usual for the people of Af Abet. Lack of water was their paramount difficulty, even in normal times. The altitude there was lower than at most SIM stations in Ethiopia. The sandy soil reminded one of the northern Sudan, which lay just over the hills to the west. Scrub bush covered the land, where goats and sheep and camels were raised.

If the rains were good, some sorghum was grown. Many of the people living around the town were nomads. They lived in portable huts made of poles and covered with palm leaf mats. When they moved to better grasslands, each "house" was loaded on a camel for the trip.

Don Stilwell and his wife, Muriel, had played a large part in opening the SIM station there. It had been hard going, but eventually the station was functioning. The medical work, headed by a nurse, was the main avenue of help to the community, the clinic was the place of greatest activity.

Don had dug a well on the property, and set up a windmill to pump from it, but often felt sorry that the supply of water wasn't greater. The waterholes dug into the dry watercourse by the local people just didn't produce enough. The mission water was shared, but that wasn't enough either.

The Stilwells were later transferred to Addis Ababa, where Don took over the SIM pharmacy. Don is a pharmacist. Ben and Ramona Motis took their place at Af Abet. Their first job was to study Tigre, the language of the area.

When the drought persisted, the village wells around Af Abet dried up completely. There was some water in the mission well, and people began to line up at the Motises' door each day for a small ration each. By the afternoon of each day, the mission well as dry, too. Sometimes up to 80 people were left with empty containers. They begged for water.

Af Abet had never been declared a disaster area, perhaps because hunger and thirst were perennial. The people came to the clinic with little flesh on their bones, and very much in need of nourishment, but famine relief supplies were not sent to Af Abet.

Nurse Elaine Douglas was happy when high protein liquid food started arriving through SIM channels so that she could give it to some of the weakest children.

Ben had often prayed for funds to use for hiring men to work on a water supply scheme. Indications were that water was there, if only they could dig deep enough for it. But it would be a big project, and a discouragingly expensive one if water was not found on the first few tries.

The missionaries established good rapport with the people of Af Abet. A small school was opened in 1972. Ben ran a sports program for the young people. One room in the school was used as a library and games room. A number of homes were open to the missionaries, and good communication was built up.

The gospel was taught as well as demonstrated. There was little hostility, but not much response either.

About the time the water shortage became critical, Chris Ott, the German nurse who had worked so hard at Alamatta and Dessie, was

sent to Af Abet to get away from the pressure of that work, and to give
the station nurse a break.

Chris had funds sent to her by friends in Germany. When she saw
the situation at Af Abet, she offered them to Ben to use in doing
something about it. Ben had a long talk with the village fathers. He
told them of the money offered, and asked if they would match it. He
would supervise the work. They agreed to raise $1000.

Ben and his crew got to work. They found water on the first try. The
people were delighted.

Then funds began to come in through R&R. More wells could be
dug.

"Do you know about the old Italian well?" Ben was asked. "They
dug it about 1935 in this same riverbed. Perhaps we can find it."

They explored the dry watercourse, eventually locating a spot where
they thought the well should be. When they had dug for a while, they
uncovered some cement. It was the casing around the top of the well.

Ben agreed to pay men to clean it out. It took four men about a
month to remove the sand and rocks that had filled it in. But it
produced sweet water, between 12 and 15 barrels a day.

But digging new wells was a tremendous problem. The layers of
rock completely frustrated the workmen. This was the major reason,
Ben concluded, that more wells had not been dug in the decades
previous. The people did not have tools to get through the rock.
Chisels and picks and shovels could never do the job.

Ben's solution was simple. He went to the Presbyterian Mission at
Ghinda, and obtained the use of their compressor and jackhammer.
He trained his workmen to use it. It was still hard going, but the rock
could now be penetrated. The men dug one well a month for six
months.

To keep the water from being polluted, Ben covered some of them,
built concrete storage tanks, and installed windmills. The people drew
from the tanks. Some of the wells which did not produce really good
water were left uncovered so the nomads could draw from them with
ropes and buckets for their animals.

There was another source of water that Ben wanted to conserve.
During the heavy showers of July and August, water came roaring
down the streams only to disappear into the sand. Ben asked for
advice, and Bob Buttenshaw was sent to look things over.

Bob was an Australian R&R worker, trained in water conservation.
He surveyed the district carefully, and selected a place where three

20. People at barren Af Abet flock to draw from a newly-dug R&R well. The well was later capped and equipped with a windmill.

21. At Af Abet, Muslims crowd into schoolroom for Sunday morning service. Before R&R water project, few showed interest. Ramona Motis in foreground.

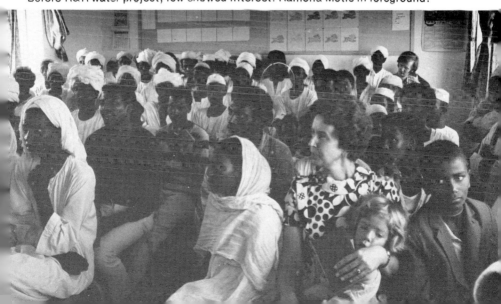

22. Well-drilling rig donated by TEAR Fund and Christoffel Blindenmission.

23. The local pump is a welcome new feature for village housewives.

24. Deep wells such as this one on the Alamatta plain will provide water even in times of drought.

25. With enough manpower, hand tools achieve wonders in road-building, a food-for-work rehabilitation program.

26. In this food-for-work reforestation scheme at Guffra, 9000 trees were planted.

27. Another food-for-work assignment was carrying supplies to places inaccessible by road. Women found this a natural kind of work.

28. Replacing oxen is one aspect of rehabilitation. Use of tractors to plow for the indigent is another.

29. R&R volunteers crowd into mission dwelling at Alamatta for meals. Most Ethiopian volunteers are Christian students.

30. R&R volunteers from overseas were teamed with Ethiopian counterparts. They were available to "go anywhere, do anything."

31. Setting up the relief camp in the mountains near Guffra. Living conditions were rugged, communication undependable.

32. Nurse Lois Mann prepares an injection at the R&R clinic near Waja, assisted by dresser Ato Sheffara.

33. At Machari clinic, nurse Heather Bobbermein had the advantage of radio communication with main base.

34. Mealtime at Adi Kai. L to R: Gloria Houston, Louise Baerg, Janice Penner, Steve Houston.

35. Don Stilwell, left, and Steve Houston Inspect the first barley crop in several years near Adi Kai, following the rainy season of 1974.

36. R&R volunteers teach literacy class at night to children at Babu Corma.

37. Using a pneumatic drill to dig the foundation for Af Abet dam.

38. An evangelist preaches to refugees at a food camp. The practical demonstration of love through R&R work ensured ready listeners. Many heard the gospel for the first time.

39. A spiritual breakthrough came at Alamatta. Being baptized here is a young man nicknamed "Eighteen I.V." because he needed 18 intravenous infusions to save his life.

streams came down the mountain and met in a narrow defile.

"An ideal place for a dam," Bob decided. "A lot of water comes down here when it rains. And it wouldn't need a long dam to back up a lot of water."

He and Ben drove around the location to see if the land could be irrigated. There were several places that could be serviced with little difficulty.

"It's a big project for us," they concluded. "But it would mean the beginning of a new era in Af Abet. It fits in well with the aims of R&R, to help prevent disaster from drought. And it would almost certainly affect the attitudes of the people here. Nobody has done anything like this for them before."

They submitted the plan to the R&R board. It was approved.

When Ben announced to the people of Af Abet that money to start building the dam had been provided, the District Officer declared a holiday. But it was a working holiday. The government offices, the school, and the hospital were to be closed. The merchants and tradesmen in the town were told to close their businesses. All the able-bodied men and boys were to gather at the site of the proposed dam.

They did. There was a great crowd gathered. On the District Officer's orders, they started to work, clearing the stream beds that ran into the pond site. Stones were lugged to the construction area. The huge trench needed for the foundation was started.

It was a happy day. The most important men of the village carried stones on their shoulders side by side with schoolboys. Af Abet had been a "famine area" long enough. This was their chance to relieve that situation.

While the men of the area worked at the dam site, the missionary women visited the village. They were greated warmly by the housewives, and invited to sit and drink tea. An entirely new attitude had come over the town. "Now we understand your talk about the things of God," one woman said. "Mr. Ben must be a man of God. He has brought us water." Ben had certainly become citizen number one in Af Abet.

There were guerrilla fighters in the hills around the town, but they did not disturb the missionaries other than to ask for medicine occasionally. It was these guerrillas, members of the ELF, who attacked the hospital at Ghinda. There was good fellowship between the Presbyterian missionaries and SIM. Debbie Dortzbach and her husband, Karl, had been loaned to SIM for relief work during the famine crisis, and had worked at the Wurgeisa camp.

Ben was laying the foundation for the dam when the news came of Debbie's kidnapping and Anna's murder. The tragedy sent a shock wave throughout Eritrea province. The Presbyterians immediately closed the Ghinda hospital and evacuated their missionaries to Asmara. Other missions agreed that they should do the same until Debbie Dortzbach was released.

The people of Af Abet were disappointed at the news that their missionaries were leaving. "Stay!" they begged. "We will not let anybody hurt you."

But the missionaries had to go. If nothing else, it was a gesture of disapproval of the kidnapping and murder. The move proved to be a wise one. The building of the dam did not stop, though. It continued under the supervision of an Ethiopian R&R worker. Remarkably, the workmen stayed on the job right through the fast of Ramadan, a major Islamic event.

In late September all the hostages were released, and the missionaries returned to Af Abet. They were warmly welcomed by the schoolteachers, the medical staff, and the people of the town. Because they had continued work on the project while Ben was away, they had come to consider it as truly *their* work. "That made our relationship even better," Ben commented.

There was a remarkably increased interest in what the missionaries had to say. "Before we started these water projects," Ben reported, "we had about a dozen, or even less, at the Sunday morning services. Now we can hardly get the congregation into the school classroom that we use as our chapel. There are sometimes over 70 there. And each morning as I hold devotions for the workmen, there are as many as 50 who join me."

Most of them were Muslims. Not a few were young men, including students. They saw the gospel at the end of a shovel as well as in the missionaries' words, and they responded.

"The school didn't do it, the clinic didn't do it," nurse Elaine Douglas explained. "Water did. The water project is the best evangelistic effort we've ever had."

17. Beautiful people

The R&R teams fanned out throughout the areas being aided by SIM. They had interesting experiences. Most of them had never been to places such as Ethiopia. They adapted well, and they learned many things.

Elspeth Slater was considered a veteran by the workers who arrived in late June and early July. She had been there for five months.

Elspeth was from Australia. When she stepped off the plane in Addis Ababa, she noticed the eucalyptus trees that grew so profusely. "Just like home," she commented. The trees were from her home. They had been introduced to Ethiopia by the Emperor Menelik, and were known in Amharic as the "trees of the sea," because they had come from across the ocean.

She was introduced to R&R work by Canadian Alex Martichenko. Alex had been with SIM since 1964. He had worked among the Somali people on the Ethiopia-Somalia border, until he had been brought into the R&R program.

Alex was tall and athletic and equipped with boundless energy. He was coordinating the work in south Wollo at the time. He drove Elspeth and her partner, Lea Nixon, to their first assignment in a four-wheel drive Toyota.

They drove past thatched houses and brown hillsides, following the great road north out of Dessie. They left the road when they came in view of Lake Haik, and were soon bouncing along the dirt road that led to Bistema.

"We had roads like this where I did nursing in the Australian outback," Elspeth said, gripping her seat. "But I don't remember being afraid of sliding over precipices!"

When they entered the town, which was built in a slight depression on top of the mountain, the children and others on the main street waved and shouted, "Alex! Alex!" Elspeth soon learned that she was working with "Alex" mission, and in an "Alex" clinic.

"This is the place we've rented for the shelter," Alex said, stopping in front of a stake fence, beyond which was an open compound and a fairly large dwelling with a corrugated metal roof. "There are about 300 people a day being fed here. And the clinic is mighty busy."

There was a great deal of shaking hands and exchanging greetings, none of which the girls understood, except for the expression, "Tenastaleen," which was the equivalent of "Hello." They made a quick tour. Then Alex drove them back into the town.

They stopped in front of an Ethiopian mud-walled house that differed not at all from the other dwellings along the narrow street. "This is the R&R house," Alex explained, and helped the girls carry in their gear.

If Elspeth had thought it might be a bit dangerous to live in such an isolated place, her fears vanished in the warmth and friendliness of the children and young people. Some of them had reached sixth grade in school, and loved to practice their English.

"Good morning," one of them said. "Where is your mother?"

In short order, the two Australian girls had answered questions about their country, their travels, and the work they would be doing. When the people heard that they were nurses, their acceptance was assured.

In the rear of the house was a room with space for two bedrolls on the dirt floor. There was no furniture.

Alex headed off to the home of the local evangelist, and returned with a basket-tray of injera and wat for their supper. It had been prepared by the evangelist's wife. This was followed by tea, served in small Ethiopian cups.

The girls put in long hours. One of their greatest frustrations was the language problem. Their dependence on translators left them feeling inadequate. Often they were unsure of themselves. They found it difficult to take advantage of opportunities to witness. By the end of a month, however, they were surprised at how many phrases and words they could hear and use.

As many other workers experienced, Elspeth became very attached to the children, in particular. There were several homeless orphans at Bistema between two and three years old. There was also Werkenish, about ten. For a time they became part of the R&R family, eating with the team members.

The team grew with the arrival of other workers, and the renting of a second house.

When Elspeth was transferred to a place called Hidi, she had another series of new experiences. That team, like the other, was composed of Ethiopians and foreigners. The team used tents.

When the people at Hidi, who were nearly all Muslims, saw the difficulties the team had living under canvas, they offered them their mosque.

The team moved in. It was only a hut, with a thatch roof and dirt floor, and sticks for walls. The sticks were to be plastered with mud some day, but at this point were open to the breeze. "Everything but privacy," Elspeth laughed. There was a covering of dry grass on the floor. It was full of fleas.

The mosque was a public building. The people were accustomed to entering it at will. The fact that it had become a home and workshop for the R&R team didn't deter them. They spent hours sitting and watching the activities of their visitors.

No matter how early they arose, the team members always had an audience to watch them wash and brush their teeth. They learned to put up with the lack of privacy when they crawled in or out of their sleeping bags, and when they cleaned their teeth and brushed their hair, but they longed for a place where they could at least have their devotions without being observed.

They sometimes retired to a rocky outcrop, but even there they were spotted by the children, who soon approached. In spite of their relentless curiosity, Elspeth loved them. "They are beautiful children," she said.

The women of the village endeared themselves to her, again at the cost of lack of privacy, when they learned that she was ill. They came and sat on the floor around her sleeping bag, while she battled with what seemed to be typhus. One woman, seven months pregnant, went to the far spring to bring Elspeth a drink of clean water. "The women are beautiful, too," Elspeth said. "They are beautiful people."

The team members gathered in the mosque each evening for Bible reading and prayer. The sheiks and other Muslims often sat nearby listening. The guitars and singing attracted them. They were full of questions. The Ethiopians on the team translated as their white friends answered questions. More often than not, however, they talked directly to the questioners, without Elspeth and her team-mates knowing what was said.

Eventually the team members felt that their presence in the mosque was being misunderstood. They didn't want to give the impression that by using the mosque they were endorsing Islam. They also longed for some privacy. They moved back into their tents.

Elspeth's experiences equipped her to answer some of the questions new workers had concerning working with Ethiopian counterparts. Elspeth had no difficulty explaining that the Ethiopians were as deeply involved and as thoroughly dedicated as any person from overseas. "They are thoughtful, they are hard workers, and they have things to hassle with that we don't," she told them. "People are always asking them to use their influence with us, as well as asking them for things directly. It's a lot easier to talk with someone who knows your language than with someone who doesn't. And a lot of them have become Christians the hard way. They've stood for Christ in places where opposition has been very real, not like the backgrounds we come from.

"And most of them are a long way from their homes, too. There are strong tribal differences in Ethiopia, and they are not always working with people of their own culture.

"They are extremely courteous and considerate. Sometimes their thoughtfulness of us is almost embarrassing."

Lack of in-depth communication with some of the Ethiopian workers was frustrating, nonetheless. Elspeth had warm feelings toward her counterpart, a girl named Ayuna. "She is a sweetie," Elspeth said. "We get on really well together. But I don't know Amharic, and she just doesn't know enough English to talk about things in depth."

Elspeth had to learn cultural things, too. On one occasion she suggested to a group of women that they should wash their clothes. "But we have only one dress," they replied. Another time she tried to explain the need of boiling drinking water, to prevent disease. "When we have boiled it," the woman asked, "where shall we keep it? We do not have extra pots."

Even such a simple thing as telling the mothers to wash the faces of the children to keep the flies from sitting on their eyes was a new concept to many. They considered the flies a nuisance, but they did not understand how they could carry disease.

Ernie Harbidge and Noel Magor were also veterans by this time. They were at Alamatta when the large group of recruits arrived. Thirty of them were assigned to work in or around Alamatta. Ernie and Noel placed them in their jobs.

Nurses were easy to assign, since there was such a great need for their services. Others were assigned to dig and cap wells, do surveys, make a summary of the oxen available, and do construction work.

One team, fresh from their crash orientation session in Addis Ababa, was sent to open a clinic at Waja. There were three young women and two young men. It was quite an experience.

The vehicle that took them out was loaded with a tent, containers for drinking water, bedrolls, cartons of medical supplies, and boxes of canned foods. There were even two camp cots. The cooking utensils were well used, and quite accustomed to being banged around on outdoor fireplaces made of stones.

Arrangements had been made for the team to use an old village house for the clinic, and another hut for sleeping. The girls chose the hut, the men pitched the tent.

In the hut, the center pole and a foot-high mud sleeping platform on one side left barely enough room for camp cots and a cooking fire. By midafternoon they were settled in, and Tesfay, the Ethiopian young man, went off to arrange for a local woman to supply them with injera and wat each day. They would live as simply as possible, and they liked Ethiopian food.

The nurses were busy studying the crowd of 30 or 40 people who had come to watch them set up camp. "Let's start using the Quack Stick," Lois suggested. "Just look at all those children. They're so thin."

The Quack Stick was named after the Quakers who had devised it. It was a system to measure undernourishment in infants and children. It showed the relationship between the height of a child and the girth of the upper arm. The upper arm girth is an accurate indication of undernourishment. Starving children often had bloated abdomens and puffy legs, which belied their true condition. The Quack Stick determined factually just how undernourished a child was.

By evening they were ready for their meal. Betty was impressed by the courteous manner of Tesfay.

"You Ethiopians are so careful and polite," she said. "You have better manners than we do."

"It is our custom," Tesfay replied.

"When you accept something from a person, you put both hands out and bow your head. If I don't receive things that way now, I feel that I have very poor manners. I'm learning a great deal from you."

"I wish we had some of this politeness in our daily lives back home," said Lois. "We're so busy we don't take time to be polite."

After supper they wandered to the paths and open areas between the village compounds and visited with the people.

"It's like Addis Ababa," Ed commented. "Everybody seems to take to the streets when they're not eating."

"Ethiopians like to be together," Tesfay explained. "Many Westerners withdraw. They gather in little family groups. We like to be out on the street or in the village. We like to talk to each other."

They went back to their hut for a cup of tea before bed. They lit candles and placed them in niches in the mud wall.

"It seems we've been here a week instead of a day," Ed commented, getting out his Bible. He read them a portion, and then each of them prayed.

Ed and Tesfay went to their tent. The whole team was ready for a good night's sleep. It was not to be.

The recruits were already used to the unearthly call of the hyenas that prowled the villages each night. They knew that hyenas killed dogs, and cats, and wild animals, and, sometimes, raided a compound for a goat or a calf. "I wonder what they do to a tent with a couple of nice young bodies asleep in it?" Ed pondered.

The hyenas did not come close that night. But other predators were waiting. The girls had difficulty getting to sleep.

"Something is biting me," Betty announced. They were all tossing and scratching. They reached for their flashlights and peered into their sleeping bags.

"Good grief!" Betty exclaimed. "Fleas!"

The three girls crawled out of their sleeping bags. "Look," Lois said, "the floor is jumping with them! Maybe that mosquito spray will fix them."

She poked through the boxes until she found the spray. The label cautioned not to use it on skin. "Toxic to humans," it read.

"It can't be any more toxic than fleas," Betty stated, and sprayed inside her bag. The other two did likewise.

There had been drought in Waja for three years. It was broken that night. Suddenly a burst of wind hit the camp, shaking the tent and the hut. The eucalyptus trees rattled their leaves. Drops of water began to fall. Soon the storm broke and rain began to drip through the rotten thatch. The girls moved their sleeping bags. They moved their boxes. They moved their medical supplies. They put raincoats over their sleeping bags and tried them again. As they lay down, they heard rustlings in the thatch.

The place was overrun with rats. "They have roads up there," Betty remarked, shining her flashlight.

"They even have cloverleaves where the roads cross," Lois added.

"They have a choir," Beth chimed in. "I'm going to light a candle. Maybe that will keep them away."

They got up again and blew the smoldering coals back into flame. Laughing at their dilemma, they put on water to boil for tea. The water had to boil for 20 minutes to kill any bacteria. The noise woke the boys in the tent.

"Are you all right?" Ed called.

"Sure, care for a cup of tea?"

By the time the tea was ready, the brief downpour had stopped, and the wind was no longer shaking the trees. By the time they finished their drink, the water was no longer dripping from the thatch.

The camp settled down. The girls took turns sleeping, one using the flashlight to keep track of the rats while the other two slept.

In the morning, the girls moved into the tent, and the boys moved into the hut.

R&R work was a valuable experience.

18. Guffra

Ross Hays was from Seattle, Washington, USA. He had completed his pre-medical training when he joined R&R for four months. He was assigned to a place called Guffra, in Wollo province.

This was a major famine area, where thousands of people were being helped. There was a clinic there, run by a volunteer nurse aided by an Ethiopian dresser.

Ross quickly recognized TB as a major disease in the area, as it was in much of Ethiopia. He discovered that it was difficult to treat, particularly since patients had to have an inoculation every day for a month, then take tablets every day for two to four years. Hardly any patient was willing to undergo that kind of extended treatment.

"People who have not been exposed to our kind of medicine can't be expected to understand the need for this incredibly long treatment," Ross told his team members. "Maybe we are unwittingly at fault, seeing as we cure so many things with one or two doses of antibiotics. They may question our ability to treat TB."

The program recommended by the World Health Organization under such circumstances was to immunize all those who were likely still free of the disease.

Since it was impossible to use laboratory methods to diagnose the many thousands of people, WHO recommended that it be assumed that all over the age 15 were either immune to TB, or had it.

Since it was not possible to diagnose all under 15, it was recommended that all under that age by given immunization shots of BCG (Bacillus Calmette Guerin).

"In this situation, with so many people weakened by famine," Ross said, "an ounce of prevention is worth a ton of cure. WHO has made BCG available, and it's an easy injection to give."

When Ross and his assistants had separated the under-15 group, he estimated that there were about 2500 around Guffra who should be immunized. They got busy.

They trekked for many days to near and distant villages, patiently explaining the program and giving immunizations. They also vaccinated many against smallpox. Questions were asked by most of those who wanted the shots. "Will I feel better tomorrow?" was a common one. Ross and his team eventually gave injections to 1900 young people and children.

Ross was much impressed by Solomon, a man who had come from southern Ethiopia to help. He was one of many who were sent by the churches there.

"It's great to have Solomon here to translate for me, and to help share the gospel," Ross said. "I wish I could learn Amharic by injection, so I could do more."

Ross spent some time checking out a large consignment of food that the government had sent to Guffra. As he looked at the huge pile. Solomon observed, "Now we are rich."

Ross reminded him that it was not their food. "We have to give it away."

"That is what it is to be rich," Solomon replied, "to be able to give away."

Ross and Solomon spent as much time as they could visiting in the villages. The people were Muslims, and most had never heard of Christ as Christians know Him. They were full of questions, which Solomon tirelessly answered. He spent long hours explaining the Scriptures.

Ross and Solomon and the other team members were thrilled to count 12 people who accepted Christ in two weeks. When Ross was reporting on these conversions, someone asked, "Why is it that suddenly we get reports from several places of response like this? It isn't because we're using different methods."

Ross agreed. "It's because the gospel seed is starting to sprout," he said. "Most of those who accepted the Lord have been working close to us. Like the two women who make injera and wat. They're with us all the time. Now the message is getting through."

When the Presbyterian hospital at Ghinda was closed because of the guerilla attack, several of the Ethiopian staff there joined R&R. One of them, Absom, went to Guffra.

Ross learned much from Absom and other Ethiopian assistants. "They taught me enough Amharic so I could get by. I could ask the patients if they had vomitting or diarrhea. They had expressions for both. It either "went out up," or "went out down." I could ask simple questions. If they answered yes or no, I was all right. If they went off into long descriptions, I was lost."

Absom showed Ross how to suture. "It felt pretty good to have an Ethiopian show me how to perform some medical techniques," he said. "One day a child arrived with a small tumor on the side of his head. Absom said, 'Do you want to take it out?' "

Ross told him he hadn't done that kind of thing before. "It's not hard. Watch," Absom replied. "We got it out," Ross recalled. "It was a beautiful experience."

A reforestation program was started, with teams of local men planting eucalyptus trees in exchange for grain. They set out 8000 plants, and reported a success rate of 90 percent. "This is a small attempt at reforestation," Don Stilwell observed, "but it proved again that small communities can play an important part in bringing about lasting improvement. Denuding the hills is a major factor in erosion, and erosion is a major problem in Ethiopia. Conservation measures such as this, once they catch on with the local people, can make a tremendous difference."

There was a rising hope around Guffra when good rains came. Crops were planted, and there was every promise of a good harvest, the first one in years. The grain was tall and forming well. Then the army worms came.

"It was pitiful," Ross reported. "People who survived that terrible famine were living in such hope. A good crop is on the way, and it is crushing to see the army worms. They eat the corn and sorghum leaves until there is nothing left. They have wiped out 50 to 90 percent of the farmers' fields."

But even with the setback in the fields, the situation at Guffra did not compare with the tragedy of the previous summer. The people who had survived were reasonably strong. The weak had died. And there was food available. People did not have to leave Guffra and beg. They did not swarm to the great road. Epidemics did not ravage them.

Work at Guffra, however, as at other places, was really just beginning. "Public health is one thing we need to get into here," Ross observed. "We keep healing people, but they go right back home and get infected all over again. If we could educate them to wash their eyes and use latrines and things like that, it would cut right down on the disease rate."

The teams did construct latrines, and tried to get the local people to use them. But few seemed to understand. So, the teams turned to those who could learn — the children. In the literacy school, good health habits were taught, along with reading, writing, Scripture, and arithmetic.

Ross could see that there was great promise in Guffra if it could be followed up. "If we can carry on our work here," he said, "we should get some trained Christian teachers who could develop the school and its curriculum. The people who have come to Christ need an evangelist or leader who can form them into a church and nourish them. They have *got* to be discipled, if they are to stand. This area has been called a closed area for years, because the people have been solidly Muslim or Orthodox. But they are open now. Perhaps the Lord had to permit famine to bring about that openness. We must not lose the opportunity."

19. Redeemed

"In famine he shall redeem thee," was the word that Eliphaz gave to Job during his time of affliction. Job could not understand why God had permitted such suffering and tragedy to come upon him.

The people of Ethiopia asked the same questions as Job. Why had God allowed drought and famine to come upon them? The answer lies in the counsel of God. But the promise of redemption shines through every human affliction. God is there. He is waiting to redeem.

Thousands upon thousands of people in northern Ethiopia heard, and are hearing, the message of redemption through faith in Jesus Christ as a consequence of famine relief and R&R. Scores of gospel messengers have taken them the good news, declaring God's offer of eternal life, and showing God's love in practical terms.

It is a thrilling experience to see hearts open to Jesus Christ. The experiences of two young men are representative of that thrill.

Larry Baum, from Ohio, USA, saw a spiritual miracle at a place called Ruga, in Wollo province. He was teamed with Fetaha Negus, a young Ethiopian about his own age. Larry had been impressed with the way God was working through R&R even before he went to Ruga. Two R&R workers had led two Orthodox priests to the Lord in Addis Ababa while Larry was there. Larry taught them John's Gospel when the other workers moved up north. One of the priests then led his sister to the Lord.

When Larry and Fetaha went to Ruga, they met similarly interested people. Most of the people there were Muslims, but they did not practice their religion seriously. "They welcomed me and came to talk to me even though I had never seen them before," Larry reported.

As Larry shared his faith with them, the people talked at length about the gospel message. He preached on Sundays, and twice a day to the crowd that gathered at the clinic.

One day Fetaha came to him. "There are several devil worshipers in Ruga. They have listened to you. They have discussed your message. They want you to go to one of their gatherings and tell them about God."

Larry didn't know what he was getting into, but he asked the Lord for protection and guidance and went with Fetaha. Fetaha and he approached the hut where the devil worshipers were gathered.

A young girl was standing outside. Fetaha translated as Larry talked with her. The girl said she was weary of being dominated by the devil. Being subject to demon powers was a terrible thing. She had had enough. She had heard the gospel at the clinic, and was ready to accept Christ. A surprised Larry explained the gospel once again and prayed with her as she gave her heart to Christ.

Inside the hut, half a dozen men and women sat on logs, leaning against the wall. They held their shawls over their mouths, as was the custom when something new was about to be spoken.

Larry felt a freedom to speak that he had never felt before. He was amazed at the ease with which he spoke to them from John chapter 10.

The oldest man in the group looked weak and sickly and appeared to be oppressed. His face bore the lines of fear. For the first time in his many years he was now realizing that it was possible to escape from the snare of the devil. With a weak but determined voice he declared,"I believe in Jesus." Then he begged for deliverance. There was immediate evidence that something had happened to him. He gave a great sigh of relief and wept copiously. Finally he stood up and spoke to his friends. Larry and Fetaha left. In the next few days, all the devil worshipers renounced Satan and professed faith in Christ.

Most of the children around Ruga had never seen a school, although they had seen their sheiks read from the Koran, which is written in Arabic. R&R workers built a mud and wattle schoolhouse. Ethiopians on the team took over the job of teaching. Soon dozens of boys and girls crowded into the schoolroom. It took months to master the 231 letters of the Amharic alphabet, but it didn't take long to learn the hymns and Scripture verses they were taught.

Before long, many of the children professed to follow Christ. That was a difficult thing to do, but there were enough adults who also made that profession to give them support.

But Larry's great concern was that these new followers of Christ be taught and nurtured to spiritual maturity. Redemption they had found. Now they needed to grow in Christ.

This was also the concern of Bruce Acer, in his work at Bistema. By the fall of 1974, this was a rather large base, well organized, with several projects. There was a clinic, a distribution scheme for sending grain by mule and camel to distant villages, a Fafa distribution program, and a food-for-work scheme that kept hundreds of men building roads.

Bruce went to Bistema to build a cistern, so the clinic would have an adequate water supply. Because Bistema was a town, the workers lived in Ethiopian houses. There was also an evangelist there, who pastored a small new congregation. Bruce had worked with The Navigators on the University of Ohio campus in USA. He knew the importance of systematic Bible study and memorization. He talked with the evangelist about his goals.

The evangelist had had very little training. He was an eager witness, and genuinely desirous to share what he knew with others. But he had had little real Bible training, and did not see his role clearly.

At first his congregation had consisted mainly of the R&R employees. As witness spread to the townspeople and some began attending the services, some were converted. Quite a few of these were women. Patients at the clinic also responded.

One day a call came from a village for help for a sick man. Bruce joined the nurse and dresser who went. It was about an hour's walk. They treated the patient and started back.

They had just begun the return trip when an older man approached them. He invited them to his home. The man was very friendly. "My name is Adam," he told them. They accepted his invitation. He showed great delight.

"My home is nothing," he said plainly. "It is not like the houses in Bistema."

Their host was excited as he showed them into his house. It was a round, thatched structure like most rural homes. He introduced his visitors to his wife, and brought three-legged handmade stools for them.

There were seven children in the family. They had once owned their own oxen, sheep, and cows, and had had good crops. Their granaries had always been full, until the famine came and swept away everything but one ox. They were just beginning to recover from the disaster, and had harvested a small crop of barley.

After drinking the coffee that was served to them, and making friends, they invited Adam to join them the following Sunday in the rented room in town that served as a church. They thanked him for his hospitality, and left.

Next Sunday as the service began, Adam appeared at the door. "It was our friendship that moved him to walk an hour to attend a gospel service for the first time in his life," Bruce concluded.

Adam listened to every word the evangelist spoke. He had never heard such a message before. All he had heard was the reading of the Koran in Arabic by a sheik. This preaching was in his own tongue, Amharic, as was the Bible which was used.

After the service, Adam invited Bruce and his friends to visit him again.

"Why not go today?" Bruce asked Tsahine, the young Ethiopian girl who assisted in the clinic. Tsahine agreed. Adam was invited to eat the noon meal with them, and then they set off for his home in the hills.

On the long walk to his home, Adam did nothing but talk to Tsahine about the things he had heard. He commented on the sermon, asked questions about it, and told her what he thought about these new truths.

Tsahine was fully equal to his questions. She loved the Lord and almost had the title "evangelist" at the clinic, where she witnessed so readily. She had led several to the Lord while treating them.

When they reached Adam's house, there was food set before them again. So great was his hospitality that he would not let them stop eating.

Tsahine drew Adam's wife into the conversation. The children listened. As she talked with them, Bruce saw them all bow their heads and pray. "They have accepted Christ as their Savior," Tsahine told them when they raised their heads.

"Under the circumstances," Bruce said, "I was pretty skeptical. But their faces had lit up, and they looked happy."

Adam sent his son outside. He returned carrying the family's only chicken. Adam gave it to his guests.

"We were overwhelmed," Bruce said. "How could we accept a gift like that from people who had scarcely enough to eat? We tried to give it back."

But Adam would not be denied the privilege of expressing his appreciation. "I have wandered in darkness all my life. Today you have brought God to me," he said. "This chicken is nothing."

Two days later, Adam appeared at Bruce's door. Wondering if something was wrong, Bruce asked him why he had walked so far.

"I have come to hear the Word of God," he said. There was no other apparent reason for his coming. Unlike some, he did not at any time ask for money or food, or favor. He came many times, always simply to hear what the Word had to say. "I do not want any of your things," he said over and over.

He almost always brought gifts, a large squash, or injera, and there were frequent invitations to visit his home again.

The people for many miles around were Muslims. Adam was the first one from his village to profess faith in Christ. The step he took brought many problems.

Bruce was soon engrossed in a discussion about next steps. "They are babes in Christ," he pointed out. "They cannot read or write. They have no teaching in their village, and no fellowship with other believers. Something must be done to teach them."

It was not long until Adam told Bruce about some of his troubles. "I used to be a bandit," he said simply. "I have robbed and killed. My neighbors have come to me because I am coming to the church here. They tell me that I should stop listening to you. Before I became a believer, I would have beaten them for interfering with my affairs.

"Then there is the matter of the ox. I have one ox. I share it with my neighbors so that all of us can have a team for plowing. My neighbors refused to lend me their ox. I could not plow. Before I became a believer, I would have beaten them for that, too. But now I am a Christian, I lend them my ox anyway."

Adam was now known for his association with "infidels." Among Muslims there is hardly a greater sin.

There was another thing that impressed Bruce. The men of the area chewed chat, as is common in many parts of Ethiopia. Each afternoon the men met together to chew the leaf and talk. The chat created a dreamy, drugged state.

Adam stopped using chat. "I don't need it any more," he said. As far as Bruce knew, he did not return to it.

"Chewing chat is really imbedded in their society," Bruce said. "When a man gives it up as Adam did, he is really separating himself from his neighbors."

Interest in the gospel continued to grow. One Sunday the "church" was full. So full, in fact, that someone took the children off for a service of their own, to make room for the adults.

When the service was over, Bruce was concerned that some of the men had not fully understood the message. It was new to them. He was especially concerned about a sheik who had come. When he asked those who wanted to discuss things further to join him, the sheik was one of five who stayed behind.

As they discussed the message, the sheik became the most interested person in the group. It was midafternoon before they broke up.

The evangelist had never before seen a Muslim who showed such interest in the Bible. He went to the sheik's house with an Arabic New Testament, and began discussion with him. The first day, the sheik read the Gospel of John. The next day he read the rest of the Gospels.

A few days later the sheik approached the house. There was someone with him. "This sheik is my friend," he explained. "He wants to discuss, too."

Bruce had some gospel pamphlets in Arabic. He gave the two men copies. They immediately sat down and read them together. They discussed the pamphlets between themselves with great interest. When they were through, the evangelist sat down with them and explained further. The eyes of both sheiks lit up as though a fire had been kindled in their minds.

"I could hardly believe it," Bruce said. "I feel quite sure the first man accepted Christ, and I think his friend did, too."

Not long after, Bruce and an Ethiopian companion visited the mosque in Bistema, and were warmly welcomed by the sheiks who had gathered for discussions and Islamic prayers. They gave their guests refreshments of sugar cane, roasted sorghum, and injera. Then followed a long period of question and answer, during which the sheiks indicated repeatedly that the famine was a punishment from God. They seemed to be searching for a way to find acceptance before Him. Two years previously missionaries would not have been permitted entrance to their mosque, under any circumstances. Now they were cordially received, and the gospel message carefully considered.

God was using the famine to speak to the people of Bistema. The message of eternal life was being heard. The same thing was happening all over northern Ethiopia.

"In famine he shall redeem thee." The ways of God are past finding out. His purposes are inscrutable. But He is present in all the affairs of this world, including the disasters.

R&R workers, SIM missionaries, and all who proclaim the glad tidings of great joy, who bind up the afflicted, who deliver the captive, and who take light to those who sit in darkness, trust Him to achieve His good purposes. They follow Him, and work for Him, and show His love, and share the good news of Jesus Christ. In His own way, in His own time, God works out His plan of redemption.

20. Home

Ali went home. He and Maryam and the boys, restored to sufficient health and strength, were given a supply of grain and helped on their way. The journey home seemed short. They went by a different route, and reached their village without exhaustion.

It was good to be home. But it felt strange, as though they had awakened after a nightmare. The house was in need of repair and cleaning. But the rain had caused the grass around it to grow, and there were patches of green everywhere.

Ali looked at his fields, where the weeds were taking over. He wondered how he would plow. His equipment, simple though it was, was gone. Ali did not know how he could replace it. But he could dig now, and he would put something into the ground.

There would be help, too, he knew. The government was helping. The mission was helping. Other organizations were helping. Seed grain was being distributed, a new kind from across the sea. It produced more abundantly than anything Ali and his neighbors had ever imagined.

A plan to replace oxen had started. If he could get an ox, Ali thought, it could be yoked with someone else's. The neighbors, taking turns, could plow their fields.

There was talk, too, of a well for the village. There was a machine, which Ali had not seen, that made a deep hole in the ground, and water came out, clean and good for drinking. Many villages were getting such wells. Some wells had an iron tower above them, with a wheel that turned in the wind. It drew the water up and put it into a

109

tank. If his village got one, Ali mused, Maryam would not have to walk to the spring. Nor would she have to use a rope and a skin bag to draw from a well. She would place her clay pot under the iron pipe, and the water would rush into it.

There was no little daughter to trot along beside her with her tiny pot, Ali grieved, and no baby to grow up and take her place, but that was in the hands of Allah.

The boys were busy exploring around the house and village. They had books now, slim volumes filled with letters that spoke to them. Ali did not hope that he could ever learn letters, but he was glad that his sons knew them. There were many things they could learn now. Maybe there would be a school nearby, too, Ali thought.

Maryam busied herself with household tasks. Their clothes were tatters. There was no bedding. She would have to get by with a pot or two, for a while. There was much to be done.

Both Ali and Maryam talked much about God. They had never really understood the Islamic faith which they and their neighbors followed. But it was the way of their people. Their fathers and grandfathers had been Muslims. Ali and Maryam had never questioned their religion.

But after their experience at the shelter, they questioned many things. Deep inside, they felt sure that the message they had heard there was true. But the shelter was behind them now. There was no way to hear the stories and songs again.

The boys read haltingly from the little papers they had received, including a Gospel of Mark. The name of Jesus was no longer strange to the ears of Ali and Maryam. The words He spoke were sweet. Ali and Maryam listened approvingly as the boys read.

But they did not give up Islam. They did not know enough about Jesus to do that. And their neighbors were still Muslims. They reviewed the ravages of famine and said, "Allah willed it." They continued the practices of their faith the same as before.

Life would soon resume its usual daily routine for Ali and Maryam, but it could never really be the same again. Too many things had happened.

Epilog: God and famine

After Ali and Maryam went home, tremendous events shook their nation. Many of the things that happened had been building for some time. The famine brought them to a head. There was dissatisfaction in the cities. There was opposition to the way the country was being run. There was great criticism of the fact that the famine had got out of hand. Turbulent scenes took place, with students demonstrating, and people striking.

On September 12, 1974, a military government took command. The ancient monarchy was dissolved, and the Emperor, Haile Selassie, was deposed. A new era began for the people of Ethiopia.

A significant new chapter began for SIM, too. The emergency famine relief measures that had begun in the spring of 1973 had expanded into the Relief and Rehabilitation program, a much larger project than had ever been anticipated.

R&R altered the course of missionary work in northern Ethiopia. It took SIM into areas where it had not been before. It opened scores of villages to the gospel message. It planted the gospel seed in the hearts of uncounted thousands of people.

The stories, already told, of Adam at Guffra, and the Muslim sheiks, and "Twelve IV, and the new believers at Fingal Guma, are only a sampling of the widespread interest and response that has been shown.

At the beginning of 1975, R&R workers were servicing 60 communities in Wollo province and 40 in Tigre. They have won the confidence of the people, and earned a hearing for the gospel. They are free to teach the Scriptures and form congregations.

SIM District Superintendent George Middleton reported 25 potential congregations meeting regularly at the end of 1974 — in a part of Ethiopia where 18 months previously there was only one SIM-related church (Alamatta), after 20 years of mission presence.

A Bible school was opened at Bora Meda early in 1974, with an Ethiopian graduate of SIM's Grace Bible College in Jimma as the principal. By the end of the year, 14 students were enrolled.

The spiritual climate of the north had changed so much that it is considered a new chapter in the history of missions there. R&R ministry is the vehicle that God used to bring this about.

R&R ministry also clinched a point that mission strategists had been studying for some time — the need for new methods in the contemporary African scene. Traditional ministries are subject to radical change or even extinction. African governments are taking over some of the things that missions have been doing for decades.

Western missionaries who want to enter African countries must satisfy governments that they can contribute to national development and growth. It is no longer possible in most African countries to get entry visas on purely religious grounds.

Rehabilitation is precisely the kind of work that African governments consider top priority.

"World food shortage is a fact of life which will affect all phases of missionary life from here on," Dr. Raymond J. Davis, SIM General Director, has told SIM missionaries. "It will be uppermost in the thinking and planning of our host countries. It is the kind of need that we, as servants of God, must endeavor to help meet. This is as appropriate a Christian service as medicine and education — as a matter of fact, in a list of priorities it might outrank them."

SIM had been involved in rehabilitation ministries in other countries, before the famine situation in Ethiopia. In Nigeria, in 1969, as the civil war over the secession of "Biafra" drew to a close, the Mission established a rehabilitation program that drew warm commendation from Nigerian authorities. It included several simple schemes, including the training of tailors to make desperately needed clothing for destitute people; training blacksmiths to make farm tools to get crops replanted; mobile medical services; and educational programs.

Those efforts were a major contributing factor in a remarkable postwar upsurge of interest in the gospel, and an unprecedented growth in new churches.

In 1972, when the civil war in Sudan ceased, SIM offered rehabilitation assistance through ACROSS (Africa Committee for Rehabilitation of Southern Sudan) and was readily welcomed by government there. It used the same kind of program as in Nigeria, and achieved excellent results.

The famine of 1973 hit West Africa, as well as Ethiopia. SIM was well established in three West African countries that were blasted by the famine. It went to work in Niger Republic, Upper Volta, and northern Nigeria.

SIM concluded that the time had come to take a new step forward. That step was the formation in Ethiopia of a new, permanent department, named Community Development.

Community Development has the same goals as the other departments, as stated in the official SIM Manual: "To preach the gospel and as rapidly as possible gather believers together into churches, preparing them to function as living organisms. Every part of the program must fit within this framework and must therefore have evangelism as the initial objective, and church planting and growth as the ultimate objective. Periodic evaluation of each activity will be undertaken by Council in light of this aim."

Community Development took over directly from R&R. It is continuing all the programs, and has made plans for consolidating gains. It has set up a five-year plan, closely related to the work and goals of the churches in Ethiopia.

Its aspects are many. It includes all projects that are directed toward the betterment of the community, with special emphasis on agriculture, health, and education. The possibilities are endless. And through all these activities is woven the presentation of the gospel and the establishment and strengthening of the church.

As has been stated, the hand of God is present in all the affairs of men, including famine. "Allah willed it," Ali and his Muslim neighbors said concerning the famine of 1973. Their attitude was typical. People of many religious persuasions, not just Islam, considered the tragedy an act of God.

"God is punishing us," many Ethiopians said. Some accepted the famine fatalistically, a few searched for the reason why God had sent it.

A local chief looked out over his people, who had come to him for their ration of government-supplied grain, and said to R&R workers,

"Why do you help us? We are starving and ill because we have sinned against God."

Such an attitude is not new. People all over the world, through all ages, have attributed such disasters to God. The history of Israel is but one example. Biblical accounts, going back to the time of Abraham, tell how famine directed the thoughts of people Godward.

In Ethiopia, the ancient Orthodox Church has preserved records of wars, famines, droughts, and epidemics. The work of priests in recording such events was largely religious.

Dr. Richard Pankhurst, in his research in this area, refers to a famine in Ethiopia at the time of Emperor Lebna Dengel, in the 16th century: "A little later, and before the Empor's death in 1540, there is a reference to the coming of a drought, as a result of which many cattle died, and there was a great fear in all the countries of Ethiopia (at this point in history, Ethiopia was not one kingdom, but many) causing the monks to send messages to Lebna Dengel, the Emperor, asking why he had sinned.

"Toward the end of the reign of Lebna Dengel there was a 'great famine the like of which had not been seen at the time of the kings of Samaria nor at the time of the destruction of the second temple, for God, in His anger, lit a fire which burned to the very depths of Siol, devouring the soil and its fruits, and He sent on the earth the teeth of animals and the venom (of serpents).'"

The so-called Great Famine in Ethiopia took place from 1888 to 1892. In non-famine times the country was covered with crops of teff, corn, barley, wheat, and sorghum. Potatoes, peas, and beans grew in abundance. Oxen were everywhere, as were horses, cows, sheep, and goats.

Streams ran down from the high mountain ranges, merging as they went and forming rivers. A prophet might have foreseen famine coming to the barren northern Sudan, or to dry, desolate Somalia. But not Ethiopia. The rains were so heavy and so regular that they provided water and silt for Egypt, thousands of miles away.

Yet the year 1888-1889 was excessively hot, Dr. Pankhurst records. Crops dried up and farmers looked out across fields from which they would get not one bushel of grain.

Martini, who later became Italian governor of Eritrea, described what he saw of the Great Famine. Starving men and women with their children set out for the coast in the vicinity of Massawa. Many of them died within sight of the city. Others built shelters of sticks and grass.

For beds they had only the hot sand.

Martini wrote:

"Here and there were abandoned corpses, their faces covered with rags. One, horrible to see, appeared to move, so swarming was it with insects which crept over the decomposing limbs in the burning sun. The dead awaited the hyenas, the living awaited death. From a thicket issued a thin murmur of voices, while hands devoid of flesh stretched forth quaking with the last shiver of life.

"Here in the sand a dying man with his last energy raises himself on his back, glares with staring, glassy and unseeing eyes, gives out a rattle and drops to the ground, striking his neck and back as he falls; there a crouching woman who can no longer speak rocks with a continuous motion a child of four or five years near to exhaustion, and devoting herself to her pallid dear one, mutters, 'Meskiin, meskiin,' (poor) in a faint, hoarse voice.

"Mothers, exhausted, heave their sucklings from the ground and follow us weeping and moaning and pointing at their shriveled breasts. We distribute some lira coins, a form of succor laughable in such indigence, useless to those who will be dead in an hour.

"I flee to escape from it and stumble on young boys searching in the excrement of camels to find a grain of dura. I flee on, horrified, stupefied, ashamed of my impotence, hiding my watch chain in shame, ashamed of myself for the breakfast I had just eaten and the dinner which awaited me."

In 1892 a cattle plague, rinderpest, appeared and added to the suffering by causing great losses of cattle. The plague was so violent that herds of animals perished in three or four days. European travelers reported seeing great areas strewn with bones of wild buffalo. Waterbuck, hartebeeste, and ibex of the desert perished.

Depopulation followed in the wake of the famine, cattle plague, and finally cholera. Bent, an English traveler quoted by Pankhurst, said of the country at large: "Civil war, famine and an epidemic of cholera have, within the last decade, played fearful havoc in Ethiopia. Villages are abandoned, the land is going out of cultivation, and wretched survivors betake themselves to the lowlands in the hope of finding employment and some means of subsistence."

Another declared that two thirds of the Galla population perished. One observed that he had been ten days' journey to the west of Addis Ababa and had gone whole days without seeing a habitation. Others who had strength to walk migrated to strange areas and eventually mixed with the local population.

In the famine of 1973-74, not many rich people or nobles were killed by the famine. Food was always available to those who could pay for it.

The tragedy, of course, is that famine happened at all. Contrary to popular belief, famine is not caused simply through lack of rain. Many semi-arid and even desert areas of the world have flourishing agriculture. Israel, scene of many famines in the past, now enjoys a stable agricultural situation, through a highly developed system of water distribution and irrigation.

In Ethiopia, as elsewhere, there were long-range causes of famine, as well as the immediate one, lack of rain. Contributing ecological factors had been accumulating for centuries. Once a land covered with magnificent native forests, large areas had gradually been stripped of trees, used mainly for firewood.

The process of deforestation inevitably led to severe water run-off during the rainy season. This, in turn, caused devastating floods and erosion. Erosion turns level farmland into gully-etched landscapes, and carries the rich volcanic soil — one of the richest in the world — down to the Red Sea on one side of the central mountains, and into the alluvial flood-plains of the Nile River on the other. In fact, the Nile Delta of Egypt owes most of its agricultural prosperity to the water and eroded soil that washes out of Ethiopia's highlands.

Maldistribution of population also has contributed to the tragedy of famine. Too-heavy concentrations of people exhaust the natural resources of an area. Family farmsteads are relentlessly subdivided, and the smaller plots are over-farmed. Nutrients are not returned to the soil.

Overgrazing is probably as critical a factor in erosion as is deforestation. Where domestic herds and flocks do not graze, Ethiopia has abundant tall grasses, even during the dry seasons. These grasses protect the soil from the clutches of wind and rain. Crop rotation is not generally practiced, leading to a concentration of grain crops and the resultant soil deterioration. Dry land farming is not much practiced. The tenant farming system causes an understandable lack of motivation among those who farm land which they do not own.

Some of the most elementary means of conserving water, such as wood lots and ponds and simple dams, are virtually unknown.

In Ethiopia, as elsewhere, protecting the ecology is the first step toward preventing drought from developing into famine with its attendant horrors.

The lesson of drought creating famine was demonstrated in West Africa, too. In fact, the world heard about the terrible conditions in West Africa before it heard about Ethiopia.

The vast area known as the Sahel, the fringe of the Sahara, had suffered the same decrease in rainfall over a period of three or four years, climaxing in almost complete failure of the rains in the summer of 1973.

Thousands of square miles were seared under the relentless sun. Unlike Ethiopia, with its soaring mountains, this, with few exceptions, is flat land. The southern and western rim of the great desert does not offer much topographical variety.

The soil is sandy. Rainfall does not compare with the torrential downpours of the tropics or of Ethiopia's highlands. About half of Niger Republic receives less than four inches of rain annually. There is no lush vegetation, such as found in the coastal areas. There is some good farmland, more marginal farmland, and much scrub, rock, and sand.

In that semi-arid expanse, subsistence is always precarious. Crops may or may not be adequate. Raising cattle and camels and sheep and goats is the preferred means of livelihood for many. About 25 percent of the total population are nomads.

Herds and flocks roam the vast expanses, grazing on the grass and scrub vegetation. Desert dwellers lead their animals in a never-ceasing search for food. In the best of seasons, the animals hold their own. In poor seasons, they become thin and scrawny.

Most farmers and semi-nomads live on one meal a day. The meal is usually eaten at dusk, or after dusk, when the heat of the day is past. When food is plentiful, the principal dish is a thick porridge, with meat or vegetable gravy. As food becomes scarcer, the gravy disappears.

Nomads live largely on animal products, notably milk and soft foods made from it. Despite the large number of animals, meat is for special occasions only. Animals are a man's wealth, not his food.

When the rains failed, the grazing lands withered and shrank. The nomads moved farther south. Those lands withered, too. Water, the most precious commodity of the desert and its borderlands, disappeared. The shallow wells of oases, and the mud holes of the rainy season water courses dried up entirely. Cattle died. People died, too.

Mass migration began. Nomads streamed southward, crowding into towns and villages in the farming belt, begging for food. But the people of the farming belt had suffered crop loss. They, too, were in need.

For the proud Tuaregs, virtual masters of the Sahara, and for the Fulanis, renowned cattle herders of West Africa, drought and famine shattered their traditional ways of life. With no land of their own, and with their camels and herds and flocks wiped out, they were totally destitute. The lords of the desert were reduced to begging.

The world rushed grain and powdered milk and medicine to aid them. SIM, at work in Niger and Upper Volta and Nigeria for years, rose to the occasion. As in Ethiopia, the Mission worked closely with SIM-related churches in distributing food and offering succor.

There was one significant similarity with northern Ethiopia. Most of the victims in the Sahel were Muslims. Islam is deeply entrenched in West Africa. Historically, the desert dwellers have all been followers of the Prophet Muhammed. Christians and pagans together make up less than 15 percent of the population of Niger Republic and pagans far outnumber Christians. Evangelical believers are a very small minority.

Islam in the Sahel has held itself aloof from Christianity. Famine changed that. The aid supplied by missionaries and national Christians opened ears and hearts to the gospel message for the first time.

Post-famine rehabilitation programs, similar to those undertaken in Ethiopia, have started a new chapter in evangelism. In addition, one of the most significant population movements in West Africa's history has taken place.

Great numbers of Fulanis have migrated southward into the middle belt of Nigeria, which contains that nation's heaviest concentration of evangelical churches. These Muslim Fulanis have "walked right into the arms of the church," as one mission leader described it.

For most of these Fulanis, their nomad way of life is over. They have been compelled to take up a more settled life style. For the first time, they are within reach of regular gospel witness.

The damage that has been done to the Sahel is enormous. Some observers feel that much of it can never be repaired. The Sahara has been steadily expanding for decades, devouring more and more of the pasture and arable land on its rim.

Its movement has been relentless, although insidious. Dwellers on the southern fringe laughed at suggestions that they and their children were in danger of slow death. Farmers and cattle herders did not recognize the danger of overgrazing. They did not know that they had more animals than the land could support.

Sheep and goats pulled the sparse grass from the soil, clump by clump. Camels denuded the trees one at a time. Nothing was replanted. Gradually the vegetation disappeared. Sand took over.

With drought, the process speeded up. Grass roots that ordinarily would have revived with a little rain, died forever. It is reported that in 1973-74, the Sahara advanced as much as 60 miles in some places.

There is no easy solution to the problems of drought and famine. To correct the misuse of the land and restore a proper balance of nature will be painful, slow, and costly. Man must pay the price of abusing God's creation.

The solution, however, whatever it may be, lies ultimately in man's relationship to God. Only when man is in harmony with his Creator will he be able to live in harmony with the creation.

God, indeed, cannot be ignored. In the beginning, He gave man a glorious and perfect world. He made him ruler of it all. The devastation and suffering that has followed has been the consequence of sin. Man has turned his back on God. He has wilfully disobeyed His laws, natural as well as spiritual. Not until the breach between God and man is healed is there hope.

That is why the message of the gospel is so important. That is why the good news of Jesus Christ is as essential as food and water. He is the light and life of the world. Only through Him can man — and creation — find salvation.

That salvation is coming. Today, the Scripture says, the whole creation is "groaning and travailing in pain," waiting for its redemption. That redemption will be effected when Jesus Christ, Lord of the universe, takes His rightful place.

The hope of the Church is truly the hope of the world, namely "the glorious appearing of the great God and our Savior Jesus Christ," and the establishing of "new heavens and a new earth, wherein dwelleth righteousness."